Black In Business

By

Talia Johnson- Huff

Copyright © 2024 - All rights reserved.

The content contained within this book may not be reproduced, duplicated or transmitted without direct written permission from the author or the publisher.

Under no circumstances will any blame or legal responsibility be held against the publisher, or author, for any damages, reparation, or monetary loss due to the information contained within this book, either directly or indirectly.

Table of Contents

Introduction 1

Chapter 1: Where I'm from 9

Chapter 2: Catching the Hustle Bug: Navigating the First Steps in Business 18

Chapter 3: Breaking Barriers: Overcoming Bias and Racism in the Entrepreneurial Journey" 31

Chapter 4: Breaking Chains: Overcoming Business Restrictions to Unlock Growth and Empowerment 47

Chapter 5: Rising Strong: Turning Adversity into Triumph 63

Chapter 6: From the Ground Up Embracing the Multifaceted Path to Self-Mastery" 69

Chapter 7: Laying the Groundwork for Your Empire" 80

Chapter 8: First Impressions: Landing Your First Customer" 92

Chapter 9: Contract Smarts: Navigating Agreements Without Getting Burned 95

Chapter10: Stretching Dollars: Mastering Your Business Budget 98

Chapter11: We're Stronger Together: Building a Support Network 104

Chapter12: Joining Forces: Crafting Meaningful Partnerships 108

Chapter13: Ballin' on a Budget: Marketing Magic for Your Business 112

Chapter14: Heart to Heart: Connecting Through Your Story ... 115

Chapter15: Rising from the Ashes: Turning Setbacks into Comebacks 122

Introduction

Welcome to "Black In Business," where I, Talia Johnson-Huff, take you on my personal journey from overcoming the odds to making it happen in the business world. But let me tell you, this book is about more than just my story. It's about us, about our journey together. It's not just for my fellow Black entrepreneurs but also for anyone who's ever dreamed of being in the black—financially speaking. We're talking about making a profit, keeping your business thriving, and not just surviving. This isn't just any book; it's a heart-to-heart with you. It shines a light on the path through the rough patches and the victories of starting something from the ground up. It's real talk, a heart-to-heart between you and me. It's about finding that inner strength, that security in who you are and what you're meant to do in this world.

And while it deeply resonates with the experiences of African American entrepreneurs navigating the tricky, often complex world of entrepreneurship, it's also a universal call to action.

It's about understanding the nuts and bolts of making your business profitable, ensuring you're not just another statistic in the long line of small, minority, women, and veteran-owned companies that struggle to stay afloat.

I'll share the ins and outs of turning what seems like roadblocks into stepping stones, especially when it comes to tapping into government contracts to boost your business. But more than that, "Black In Business" is an open invitation to you to learn the art of staying in the black, ensuring your venture doesn't just add to the diversity of the business world but also to its economic strength.

WE ARE DREAMING BIG, OWNING OUR OWN POWER, and let's carve out our own success stories in the business realm together. Whether you're just dreaming about starting your own thing, you're already in the game looking to level up, or you're focused on ensuring your business is financially healthy and profitable, I'm talking to you.

So, grab your pen, your journal, and your favorite drink, head over to YouTube, and vibe out to the sounds of Marja'e. It's Getting Real. We're about to dive deep into a journey from my early days to the pivotal moments that defined my career; this book is a guide to thriving, not just surviving, in the business world. Not just by starting your venture but by ensuring it's a beacon of financial success and stability. Let's show the world what it means to be fierce in the face of challenges and to turn every setback into our biggest comebacks, all while keeping our businesses firmly in the black.

This is personal because that's what business is at its core - a reflection of who we are and what we believe in.

I've got tears in my eyes thinking about how the words on these pages will touch your heart and spark something amazing inside of you. I'm excited for you to find your footing. Do you have that burning desire down inside of you to do more, but it seems like no one can feel it but you? This is the book that comes to affirm you.

YOU HAVE FOUND YOUR TRIBE! AND NO, I'M NOT THE LEADER! WE ALL ARE!

I recognize the leader in you because you felt it in your heart to read THIS BOOK!

This is a space for us to explore, grow, and get real about what it takes to be successful, not just in business but in life. It's culturally rich, full of stories and lessons that resonate with our community, but open and welcoming to anyone who's on this path with us. Our business, our hustle—it's personal. It's like raising a child; it needs love, attention, and a whole lot of patience. And just like any good parent, I'm here to guide you, to help you nurture and elevate your "baby" into something phenomenal. So, as we move forward, remember that this is a shared experience. We're building something that lasts, ensuring that you're as secure in your business as you are in yourself. Let's make this journey together, lifting each other up, learning from one another, and creating something truly special. Welcome to our shared journey of growth, empowerment, and success.

Let's dive into the real talk. And by real talk, I mean the kind that makes you laugh, think, and maybe even wanna call your cousin and say, "Girl, you won't believe what I just read!"

Let's ELEVATE!

As I told you earlier, I'm Talia...no scratch that out.

My name is Talia Huff... wait, people don't know me by that name, and it sounds more professional if I utilize my full name, so...

Let's just go with Talia Johnson-Huff. OK, that's better! That will satisfy my dad because I am still his daughter, and he helped me a whole lot along the way. My mother will be happy that I still choose to keep my last name because you don't let no man come along and change who you are, but then it'll also satisfy my husband, even though he begged me not to hyphenate my last name, but I make the excuse that I need to keep Johnson for business purposes. At the same time, I don't need a man's last name to validate me or make me who I am because being married is a prize or a 1st place ribbon in the race to beat my sister or brother at love and companionship! We all need friendly competition, right?

Alright, now that we've got the name situation all sorted out (phew, that was a whole thing, wasn't it?)

Let's jump into this self-help book!!!!

What?!

Why is your face all scrunched up?

You're not ready to jump in?

Ohhhh... you have some issues with the dialog above?

Listen, I just don't want any problems with my family, and I have to keep my husband pleased as well because, at this point, it's all about them and less about me because FAMILY IS EVERYTHING! Being married is what I'm supposed to do, and it's what I was taught. Y'all don't get it! Y'all don't understand me! See, I'm different! My family is tight, and we have to always make sure... never mind.

I'm explaining myself too much; let me just tell you my story, and then we can jump into this business stuff because that's the important part. Okay, so boom.

Here I am, standing at the intersection of being my own woman and carrying around a bunch of names like I'm trying to win a scrabble game. But let's get something straight: while family and marriage are big parts of who I am, they are not the whole story. And this is something a lot of us, especially women in the Black community, wrestle with. We're often taught from a young age to keep everyone happy. Your dad wants you to carry the family name like it's a badge of honor, your mom wants you to remember where you came from, and your husband... well, he's got his own ideas about names and roles.

But here's the deal: trying to please everyone can have you running in circles, losing sight of what you want for yourself. And let's not even start on how this plays out in business. You try to be everything to everyone, and before you know it, you're bending over backwards, losing out on deals, and forgetting why you started your business in the first place. People pleasing in business is like trying to fill up everyone else's cup while yours is running dry. Spoiler alert: IT DOESN'T END WELL!

But we're going to unpack all of that. We're going to explore just how weighed down you can become when you're too busy trying to make everyone else happy. We're going to talk about the importance of setting boundaries, both in your personal life and in your business. Trust me; we'll have some laughs along the way because if we can't laugh at ourselves, then what are we even doing?

Now, about this whole "property of your husband" business. Let's get one thing clear: marriage is a partnership, not a property transfer. Just because you're married doesn't mean you lose your identity or become someone else's accessory. We're celebrating being strong, independent women who can be in loving, supportive marriages without losing ourselves in the process. With all that we just went through together, I think we should go ahead and jump into our first lesson:

Lesson 1: Healing from "People Pleasing"

People pleasing is when you put the needs of others ahead of your own. You may hear people say things like "You're so helpful" or "You always agree with me". It is nice to be nice, but there is a fine line between being nice and always wanting the approval of others. Have you been in a situation where you may have done something you really did not want to do? For example, I remember I had a friend who always wanted to go out, and I'm really a homebody. I'd tell her that I was going to stay in the house and get some work done, but she'd come over anyway. She knew that I'd eventually cave in and go out just because I didn't want her to feel bad. I struggled with, and I still struggle with, People pleasing. Over time, I have learned to set boundaries for my own sanity.

If you're feeling uncomfortable at this point, it may be because I just called out your struggle. My goal is to challenge you. Let's talk about this. See, earlier, you were laughing at me for struggling with the very same thing, but when I call you out, you're uncomfortable. Ha, I bet you won't laugh at my struggle next time. I still love you, though.

So how do we heal from "People Pleasing"?

1.   Recognize that it's okay to put yourself first sometimes. It's okay to say no, to have your own dreams and ambitions, and to pursue them with all the fierceness you've got.

2.   Know your limits and communicate them. Be clear and specific about what you are willing to say yes to.

For those of you who are out there feeling the pressure to keep everyone else happy, remember this: your happiness matters too. It's not selfish to take care of yourself; it's necessary.

There is a bit of a method to my madness. I know some are wondering why I started a "Business Book" talking about people pleasing, and because I am a nice person, let me tell you that "People Pleasing" will affect your business, especially your money. One of the biggest challenges for black-owned businesses is having access to capital (money). While "People Pleasing" is not the main reason, it certainly weighs in, not far, from the number one position. Doing things like purchasing items that you are unable to afford so that you can "look" the part, "People Pleasing". Treating/paying for family and friends all of the time because people equate being in business to having money in the bank, "People Pleasing". Giving free products or services to our homeboy so that you can feel like the "big dog", "People Pleasing". I think you get the idea of what I am saying without saying it out loud. I'm heavy on the "not putting my people on blast".

Keep in mind that this book is about finding balance, embracing your individuality, and building a business that reflects who you truly are. It's about understanding that you can love and support your family and friends and still carve out space for your dreams.

Now that we've got all of that out of the way, are you ready to dive into this next part of the book with me? Great! Because we've got a lot to cover, and I promise, it's going to be a ride you won't want to miss. So, let's get started, and remember: be you, do you, for you.

Chapter 1:

Where I'm from

We started in a rough part of town, in the heart of a neighborhood that's seen more than its fair share of hard times. In the kind of neighborhood where you'd find the corner store that feels like a community hub, where a kid could run errands for their mom, picking up a mix of groceries, beer, and cigarettes, all on the strength of a handwritten note.

In the kind of neighborhood where my mom, scarred by the traumas of her past, found solace in drugs, a choice that cast long shadows over our childhood.

You see, growing up here wasn't easy. It was like living in two worlds at the same time. On one side, you had the hard realities of life staring you in the face – from folks struggling with addiction to the everyday hustle just to make ends meet. Then on the other side you had hope. Hope because that is what you learned to have by going to church.

Speaking about my mom, she's had her share of battles. Life threw some pretty tough punches her way early on. Sadly, it's a story too common in our communities. Did you know that studies show African American families are hit harder by substance abuse, partly because of the lack of access to proper treatment and support? Yeah, it's a cycle that's tough to break, and it's something we live through every day. Even in the midst of her own struggles, she was babysitting everyone's children. Everyone lived with us when they needed help, from my pedophile cousin, who I won't give the satisfaction of discussing, to my cousin, who had a long and deep battle with drugs himself and has since cleaned himself up to become a contributing member of society. My mom's story is one of pain, heartache, and misunderstanding but also of triumph, strength, and perseverance, which I will let her tell on her own time and in her own way.

On the other hand, my dad was out there chasing the American Dream with every tool he had. He wasn't just building his business; he was building a legacy. But with him always working, we hardly ever saw him. Yes, we were those kids who would get dressed because it was our dad's weekend, and then we're sitting on the couch in full snow suit waiting for him to come, not letting our mother put us to bed because daddy was coming, and he'd never show up. My brothers resented him for that, but me, I had hope that he was coming, because I was told that hope can fix it. Sadly, that hope did not bring my daddy to pick me up. I can laugh about it now, but back then it was not funny. When he did come, it was like a mini celebration. He'd roll up in his box truck, decked out with the logo of his plumbing and heating company – a symbol of black entrepreneurship in a neighborhood that didn't see much of it. That truck wasn't just a vehicle; it was a rolling testament to what we could achieve, if we ever stepped outside of the family. Even if it meant we'd have to live on the better side of town, like my dad did, with my wicked stepmother who did not care for me as a kid. Fortunately for me, and unfortunately for her, that didn't turn out well for her.

Living in this kind of environment, you learn a lot about resilience and the importance of community. You see the struggles, but you also see the strength. Families might not always stay together, and the stats are there to back it up – with high divorce rates and single-parent homes more common among African Americans. But even then, there's this incredible ability to keep pushing forward, to build something out of nothing. And if we're being honest, some of the reasons that our parents got divorced was because of the harsh realities we lived in but also because of the people that put their noses where they didn't belong. Later in life, my mom told the stories of her and my dad, and she secretly still loves him, but they have mutual respect for each other. Who knows what could have been had my mom received the proper counseling services and my dad not had scars because of who his mom was and how he grew up? We have no clue how "healed" marriages can make the world a better place because, in healed marriages and families, creativity expands and becomes something beautiful, which can also happen in the midst of adversity, so there's that.

And then there was Terry, my mom's boyfriend, a man wrestling with his own demons but somehow finding the strength to be the guardian we needed. Terry, with his handyman skills and a knack for fixing up houses, introduced me to the world of construction. He taught me practical skills, from driving a car to the proper way to devour chicken wings, lessons my father never had the chance to impart. Terry, a towering figure with a Southern drawl, was our makeshift sensei, convincing my brother he was the next karate master with his impromptu lessons in kicks and punches.

Our Saturdays were adventures, with Terry leading the way, my brother and I in tow, ready to take on the day's work. It was our introduction to entrepreneurship, our first taste of what it meant to earn our keep. Through Terry's eyes, I saw the blueprint of a business owner, flawed but striving, teaching us that success was as much about the effort as it was about the outcome.

This complex tapestry of relationships and experiences shaped us in ways both profound and subtle. Growing up in a home marked by separation, addiction, and the absence of traditional parental figures, I learned to navigate the world through the examples set by the adults in my life. For me, Terry's influence was pivotal, instilling in me a sense of purpose and a drive to succeed despite the odds. Even more odd than that is Terry was a beacon of hope in all of this chaos. I knew that he loved me and that he would do anything for me. I knew that bit because, for Christmas one year, some poor little girl had all of her Christmas gifts taken from her home. Well, that little girl wasn't me because he was the one who stole them so that my eyes would be bright with Christmas cheer, and I would find that out later in life. Talk about irony.

This story isn't just about the challenges; it's about finding those glimmers of hope and learning from them. It's about understanding that success isn't just about what you achieve but about what you overcome to get there. As we move through this book, I'll share more about how these experiences shaped me, how they influenced my view on success, family, and how I do business.

So, as we turn these pages together, think of it as a journey through the highs and lows of growing up in a neighborhood that taught me more about life than any classroom ever could. It's a story of pain, yes, but also of triumph and the unbreakable spirit of a community that refuses to be defined by its struggles. I learned a lot from that community and actually transitioned back into that community as an adult. I moved around a lot as a kid, and my grandparents weren't too fond of that, so they decided to make a change/ shift.

Moving day was exciting because my grandparents, who were Pastor and First Lady, made the decision that they were buying a home large enough for my mom, myself, and my two brothers to move into. They were not leaving us in that part of town with my mom on drugs and their hearts beating out of their chests with worry. Them making that decision was the best thing that happened to me. When we went for the walk-through of the new house, although the cabinets were old and the flooring needed to be changed, it was dope. We walked through as a family, following behind my grandfather as he took the cross and slung blessed oil all over the floors, walls, cabinets, and doorways. Nobody asked who was going to clean it up, but it was a thought that kept crossing my mind the entire prayer; plus, I was hoping none of us slid across the floor from getting that blessed oil on the bottom of our shoes.

We were a tight family unit. I only have one biological aunt, no uncles and we all lived around the corner from our other family members. The chain of command was that you ask your mom, then ask your grandmother, and then you have to ask your aunt because she is the one who is street smart and knew if you were trying to run a game on her. You heard me mention the fact that I lived in the house with my Pastor grandfather and first lady grandmother, that instilled in us that GOD and FAMILY IS EVERYTHING.

So, you should have a better understanding of the dialog you and I had earlier when you first began reading this amazing book.

Living in that new home, blessed from corner to corner, was the fresh start we desperately needed. This move wasn't just a physical relocation; it was a spiritual and emotional journey towards stability and a semblance of normalcy, or so I thought. This neighborhood posed its own set of problems that followed me well into adulthood. It was a "better" part of town, if that's what you want to call it. Well, put it like this: I'm a girl from around the way. What do I mean by "Around The Way"? Well, my around the way may not be your around the way, but where I grew up, in my early teenage years, was not exactly the ghetto, but it was not the suburbs either. Growing up in what I like to call the "ghetto suburbs" presented a unique set of challenges and experiences. It was a place where the lines between right and wrong, sacred and secular, were constantly blurred. My home was rooted in Christianity, a beacon of faith in a neighborhood that seemed to navigate by a different compass. Sundays were for church, and every other day was for living out those teachings as best as we could amidst the realities of our surroundings.

But outside the protective walls of our home and church, the streets told a different story. There was Miss Lisa, known by everyone as the woman who seemed to have a revolving door for the men in the neighborhood, married or not. Then there was Mr. James, the too-friendly man whose gaze lingered a little too long on the young girls passing by. These were the characters of my childhood, the subjects of hushed conversations I wasn't supposed to hear but did, the real-life examples of what our Sunday school teachers warned us against.

I was always observing, always listening. I found myself often nestled under the protective wing of the church elders, absorbing their wisdom, their judgments, and their hopes for a saved soul or two. They spoke of salvation like it was a shield against the very streets we called home, a barrier against the temptations that lay just outside our front doors.

Living a Christian existence while being surrounded by those who didn't share the same values was like walking a tightrope. At school and around the neighborhood, the pressures were different. There were parties I wasn't allowed to attend, music I was forbidden to listen to, and a whole host of "worldly" activities deemed off-limits by my upbringing. Yet, the allure of those forbidden fruits was ever-present, a constant test of faith and obedience.

In this setting, I learned the art of balance and the importance of making choices. It wasn't about judging Miss Lisa or Mr. James; it was about understanding that everyone's path was different and that mine was guided by the principles instilled in me from a young age. But understanding didn't make it any easier to navigate the complexities of growing up with one foot in the church and the other dying to step out into the world.

As I matured, the stories and lessons from those early days stayed with me. They became the foundation upon which I built my identity, not just as a Christian but as a young black woman striving to find her place in a world that often seemed at odds with everything she was taught to value. The "ghetto suburbs" was my classroom, a place where faith, resilience, and the reality of life intersected in ways that textbooks and sermons could never fully capture.

This narrative, this slice of life from the "ghetto suburbs," sets the stage for a journey of self-discovery, of wrestling with questions of faith and morality against the backdrop of a community rich with characters and challenges. It's about finding my own voice among the many expectations, societal norms, and personal beliefs. It's a story many of us know all too well, a story that resonates with anyone who's ever had to balance the teachings of Sunday morning with the lessons learned on the streets where they grew up.

Fast forward through the trials, the errors, and the lessons learned; each experience was a building block towards my future. From my early days braiding hair to navigating the complexities of family expectations and societal norms, every moment was preparing me for my ultimate calling: entrepreneurship. The business itch that began with a fascination for hair extensions evolved into a profound understanding that business is about solving problems, creating value, and making connections.

Chapter 2:

Catching the Hustle Bug: Navigating the First Steps in Business

In this chapter, we dive headfirst into the 'Business Itch' — that undeniable, burning desire to create something of your own, to step into the world of entrepreneurship with hopes and dreams packed tightly in your toolkit. It's about that initial spark, the one that keeps you up at night, plotting and planning, dreaming of building an empire from the ground up. But what happens after the spark? How do you turn that itch into a reality?

We'll unravel the mysteries of pricing your products or services — because, let's face it, even the greatest business idea won't get far if the numbers don't make sense. Pricing isn't just about covering costs and slapping on a profit margin; it's an art. It's about understanding your worth, knowing your market, and valuing your offer in a way that speaks to both.

And then there's the big question: What makes a real business? Is it having your name on a door or a product on the shelf, or is it something deeper, more intrinsic? We'll explore the essence of entrepreneurship beyond the paperwork and the bottom line. It's about impact, solving problems, and filling gaps. It's about creating something that matters, not just to you but to the community you serve.

This chapter sets the stage for a journey of discovery, learning, and growth. It's for anyone who's ever felt the 'Business Itch'—the aspiring entrepreneurs, the dreamers, the doers. Whether you're scribbling ideas on a napkin or laying the foundation for what's next, this chapter is your starting line. Let's tackle the challenges, celebrate the victories, and transform that itch into a thriving, vibrant business.

You are probably trying to figure out when is the best time to take notes, NOW, duh?

Back when I was about 12, I caught what I like to call the "business itch." You know that strong feeling that pushes you to go after something even though you know it won't be easy? Yeah, that's the one. For me, it all started with beauty, specifically hair. In the 90s, when I was growing up in Buffalo, there were a few hair stores around. One of my favorite spots was Mid-K. They had shelves stacked with all kinds of hair products, and I was obsessed. I couldn't get enough of the idea that you could completely change your look just by switching up your hair. You could add straight extensions, wavy extensions, curly extensions, you name it. But what really got me excited was the color.

Now, let me tell you about my "auntie." She wasn't actually my aunt, but she was my aunt's best friend, and she was a wizard with hair. I used to sit in her kitchen and watch her work her magic on all sorts of women. It wasn't just about making them look good; she was like their therapist too. They'd pour their hearts out to her while she worked her hairstyling magic. And I wanted in on that. But I wasn't talking about the simple stuff like wetting your hair on

Easter and hoping for cute curls that only lasted an hour. No, I'm talking about the fancy finger waves, the intricate braids, the works.

Picture it: a cozy kitchen buzzing with the sound of gossip and laughter, the smell of hair products lingering in the air like a sweet perfume. My "auntie", she's at the center of it all, working her magic with a curling iron in one hand and dishing out juicy gossip with the other. Her clients are spilling their secrets like they're passing around a collection plate at church. There's talk about who's seeing who, who got caught doing what with who – you know, the good stuff. And my auntie, she's just like a therapist in a hairnet, listening intently, nodding sympathetically, all while weaving intricate designs into her clients' hair.

And me? Well, I'm perched on a stool in the corner, wide-eyed and fascinated by it all. I watch as the cash exchanges hands – some paying upfront, others promising to pay later. And then there's the bartering. Oh, the bartering. It's like a dance, a delicate negotiation between my auntie and her clients. "I'll do your hair now, and you can help me with my groceries later," she'll say with a sly grin, and they'll nod in agreement, sealing the deal with a handshake.

But amidst all the chatter and laughter, there's a lesson to be learned. It's about more than just braids and curls – it's about community, trust, and hard work paying off. My auntie may have been a master with a curling iron, but she was also a savvy businesswoman, building her empire one client at a time, although there was usually several waiting in line. So, as I sat there, soaking it all in, I knew that one day, I wanted to be just like her – a pillar of the community, a trusted confidante, and a damn good hairstylist. And thanks to her, I knew exactly where to start.

My specialty didn't begin as extravagant as that, which it would one day, but I began braiding. Yes. I could throw a quick weave in someone's hair by the age of twelve and use the Marcel irons like I was a veteran master stylist, but braids paid me more money, and people trusted the 12-year-old to install their micro braids. I charged $80 for a full head of micro braids that would take me two days to complete. Of course, I didn't work sunup to sun down; it was more of the weekends, after school schedule, so I basically took about 8 to 10 hours to complete a full head of micro braids, which would be about $8 to $10 an hour for a 12-year-old girl. That was more than minimum wage back then, so I was doing well. Not to mention, I didn't have any overhead (Cost to do business). There was no social media back then, so I had nowhere to post my work, but I made sure that my clients were happy, so they'd tell their friends and families about me. This grew my little "hobby" into a pretty thriving small business. So, what do we know so far that you could have taken notes on?

We spoke about several things, and these are the "things" that should keep you going on your journey, when all else seems to fail. You want to go back to these when you're experiencing the burn out, the loss of passion, the sleepless nights, the low funds and the rough patches in business.

1. The first, most important, thing that I NEVER want you to forget is your WHY? The "WHY" is your inspiration.

2. Defining the Business Itch: I've always said that the "Business Itch" is knowing deep down you have to do something, not just thinking you should. It's when an idea grabs you and won't let go. This is important because you need to understand the difference between something you think you should do and something that you know that you know you want to do because you can't stop thinking about it—the itch Baby doll. The INSPIRATION for me was seeing my aunt in the kitchen, using her talent, her tools and her beautiful personality to pave the way for her entrepreneurial journey. To this day, she still does hairstyling, and her business has evolved into so many different areas, including ministry.

4. Choosing Your Niche: We all have so many talents and while I was able to perform a wide array of different hairstyles, out of all the hairstyles, I gravitated towards one specific technique. Finding that one thing that can actually make you money, is crucial.

5. Your Money: This goes hand and hand with remembering your "Why". Just as much as you remember why you do what you do, you need to remember that one of your whys is to feed your passion. Your passion has to eat. In order to move that business forward, we must know about our money. I gave you the amount of money that I was able to make performing the service and how long it took me to perform the service. I gave you a way to calculate your price and break it down so that it makes dollars and sense.

6. Marketing and Customer Service: We must know how we are going to let people know what we do, so that we

can get them to our product or service. My strategy for getting the word out and making sure clients are happy was key to my success. Remember, how you treat your customers makes all the difference. I explained my marketing strategy (plan of action designed to promote and sell a product or service) and how it helped my business thrive. I told you that customer service was key (the way a company/business treats the people who buy or uses its products or services.)

So back in the day, when I was knee-deep in hair extensions and vibrant colors, I didn't just stumble into entrepreneurship – I dove headfirst into a world where beauty and business collided. Those early days weren't just about braids and curls; they were about building something bigger, something that went beyond hairdos and turned into an experience. See, I realized early on that running a business wasn't just about making money – it was about creating connections, about making people feel seen and heard. My little hair venture taught me some big lessons: it's about finding what you love and turning it into your hustle, about knowing your community and serving them well.

As my little business grew, I saw firsthand how important it was to stay true to your roots, to understand the needs of the people around you, and to always deliver top-notch service. It wasn't just about making a buck; it was about making a difference.

And that's what laid the foundation for MWBE Constructors, Inc. – a company built on passion, dedication, and a deep understanding of what it means to truly serve your community. My journey, and the journeys of so many others in the game, taught me that success isn't just about the money – it's about knowing your 'why,' perfecting your craft, and never backing down from a challenge.

So, as we close this chapter and move forward into the next,

There may be a couple of you who feel that my little business wasn't really a business because it was never incorporated, and I never filed taxes. You are partially correct, but that leads me to a question I'd like you to answer for yourself.

What is business to you

_____

_____

I leave you this space because business is different for everyone, but it has to mean something to you, the "Business Woman", the "Business Man". Now, the textbook definition of Business is a person's regular occupation, profession or trade. Then, there is this version of business, which is the regular production or purchase and sale of goods undertaken with the objective of earning a profit. To me, business isn't just about the formal setup, although we are here to ensure that your business is setup properly, it's about the hustle and the drive. By that definition, was I running my hair braiding gig at 12? Absolutely, I was in business.

With that being said, let's talk about cash flow. Because understanding your cash flow is like knowing the secret ingredient in your grandma's famous recipe—it's crucial. When I started braiding hair at 12, charging $80 for a full head of microbraids, I was making more than some adults. But let's break it down, shall we?

Understanding Gross Profit and Net Profit

Gross profit, in simple terms, is what you make before you subtract all the costs of doing your business. For me, my gross profit on each head of micro braids was that sweet $80. Now, net profit, that's what you have left after you take away all the expenses. Luckily, my expenses were low—no rent for a salon chair, no utility bills, just the cost of hair and maybe some snacks to keep me going. So, if I spent $10 on hair supplies, my net profit was $70. *See how that works?* It's like knowing exactly how much you're really making after everything's said and done.

The Importance of Marketing

Back in the day, marketing was all about word of mouth. No hashtags, no social media shoutouts. If your work was good, people talked. If it wasn't, well... people talked even more. The lesson here? Always bring your A-game because happy clients are your best advertisers. They're the ones who'll keep your phone ringing and your schedule packed.

Sacrifice and Hustle

Building a business, even a small one like mine, required sacrifice. It meant giving up weekends and after-school hours to braid hair instead of hanging out. But here's the thing—those sacrifices pay off. They teach you discipline, time management, and, most importantly, they show you that hard work can lead to success.

Profit and Loss Statements

Now, onto something a bit more technical but super important: profit and loss statements. Think of this as a report card for your business. It shows how much money you're making (income) and how much you're spending (expenses). Why is this crucial? *Because it tells you if your business is healthy*. If you're spending more on hair products than you're making from braiding, that's a problem. It's like keeping score, ensuring you're always on the winning side. People in business have made this sound way harder than it is because they want to stay ahead of you. Knowing and understanding your *Profit and Loss statement* is what will make the difference between money in the bank and no money in the bank. Banks, credit unions, and loan agencies will ask you questions that will gauge YOUR understanding of YOUR business. If *you* have no clue about *your* financials, how can they trust *you* to pay them back the money that they have lent out to *you?* **Pro Tip: Have your accountant or someone that you know and trust who works in the financial world explain the Profit or loss statement to you. If you are unable to find someone who will explain it to you, go into your local bank branch and ask your relationship manager if there is someone who can break it down for you*** Don't stay ignorant; get the knowledge that you need.

Costs of Products and Services

Knowing how much your service costs is vital. Calculating how much I spent on hair supplies against what I charged for microbraids helped me understand my profits. This is key for any business, especially for minority and women-owned businesses. We often start with less capital, so every dollar must work hard for us.

Alright, **let's break down pricing your products or services in a way that's super simple and straightforward**, kind of like explaining how to make the best sweet potato pie without leaving out any of the secret spices. I'm going to give you a couple of examples because the more you read each scenario, the more you will understand. Another tip that I want to share is "WRITE THINGS DOWN". It's important to write because what you are writing is subconsciously submitted to your memory.

When it comes to setting prices, it's all about making sure you're not only covering your costs but also making a profit (that's the extra money you get to keep).

Think about it like this:

Imagine you're selling lemonade in your neighborhood. You've got to buy lemons, sugar, and water. Now, if those ingredients cost you $5 and you sell the whole jug of lemonade for $10, your profit is $5. Easy peasy, right?

Big Companies vs. Your Hustle

Big companies, like those fancy coffee shops that sell lattes for $5 a cup, have a bunch of folks sitting in offices crunching numbers on computers to figure out their prices. They consider the cost of coffee beans, milk, and even the cup and lid. Then, they add a bit extra to make sure they're making money after paying their employees and keeping the lights on.

But here's the deal: You don't need fancy software to get your pricing right. If you're running a smaller business or offering a service like hairstyling or lawn care, you can still price your services smartly.

How to Price Like a Pro

1. Know Your Costs: First, know exactly how much it costs to offer your service. If you're a hairstylist, *how much do you spend on hair products for one client?* If you're mowing lawns, *how much does the gas for your mower cost per lawn?*

2. Check Out the Competition: Look around at what others are charging for similar services. You don't want to be the most expensive (unless you're offering something extra special), but you don't want to be the cheapest either and shortchange yourself.

3. Time is Money: Consider how much time it takes you to provide your service. If it takes you 2 hours to do a hairstyle and you want to make at least $15 an hour for your work, you need to charge at least $30, plus the cost of your products.

4. Add a Little Extra: Once you've covered your costs and paid yourself for your time, add a bit more to the price. This extra is your profit. It's what you use to grow your business, save for a rainy day, or treat yourself for all your hard work.

5. Keep It Simple: You don't need a calculator for every decision. Round your prices to make them easy to remember and handle. If the math says you should charge $47.50, consider making it $50. It's easier for you and your

customers, at least until you can afford the proper pricing software.

More Examples

Let's say you bake cakes. Your ingredients cost $20, and it takes you 4 hours to make a cake. You want to pay yourself $15 an hour, so that's $60 for your time. Add that to your ingredient cost, and you're at $80. Now, add a bit more for your profit—let's say $20. So, you'll charge $100 for a cake. This price covers your costs, pays you for your time, and gives you a little extra.

Final Sip

Pricing doesn't have to be complicated. It's about knowing your costs, understanding what your time is worth, checking out the competition, and then making sure there's a little left over for you. Whether you're baking cakes, styling hair, or fixing cars, the same basic rules apply. Keep it straightforward, and you'll be on your way to pricing your products and services like a boss.

Let's Chat!

How are you feeling about these financial basics?

Do you see how understanding money can make a *huge* difference in your business?

Let's take a moment to reflect. *What's one financial goal you have for your own hustle?*

Share your thoughts, and remember, every big business started with someone, somewhere, making that first smart money move.

And although I'd love to tell you that this is all that you need to know as an entrepreneur, I'd be lying to you. There is so much more to uncover. The big problem in my childhood business was that I had no plan. Although I wasn't doing it for the money, I wish that someone would had taught me how to price and to write a business plan, and maybe I would've opened my first salon or started a mega business doing hair weave or anything other than just hope and pray for the next phone call. Some of these women knew and understood how much I was saving them, but none in my family told me about profit and loss, how to prepare a business plan that's ready for funding, or even how to set my business up properly. I truly wish that I had that knowledge then, but I do now, which is part of the reason I am writing this book. I hope you are taking notes because writing things down helps the information stick in your brain, as I told you earlier. I now use my remarkable, which is an amazing tool for your business. It helps me keep things organized without having to carry around 90 notebooks or remember what color notebook I used for what project.

In this next little chapter, we're going to talk about some of the things that come against us in business. This is so that you are prepared for anything that may be thrown your way. I understand that we may come from different backgrounds, but many of us face some of the same challenges, and that is where this chapter is going to come in handy for you.

Chapter 3:

Breaking Barriers: Overcoming Bias and Racism in the Entrepreneurial Journey"

In "Breaking Barriers: Overcoming Bias and Racism in the Entrepreneurial Journey," we're getting transparent about the struggles many of us face as entrepreneurs, especially those of us who come from minority backgrounds. This chapter isn't just about swapping stories; it's about tackling a problem that's been holding us back for way too long.

Let's be honest – being an entrepreneur is tough for anyone, but for folks like us – people of color, women, veterans – it's like climbing a mountain with no gear. We're facing bias and racism at every turn, like invisible walls blocking our path to success.

It's about dealing with people who don't think we belong in the boardroom, or who assume we can't handle the pressure. It's about having to work twice as hard to prove ourselves, just because of the color of our skin or our gender.

And let's not even get started on the funding game – it's like trying to play poker when the deck is stacked against you from the start. Bias and racism in business can show up in all sorts of ways, from subtle digs to outright discrimination. It's exhausting, frustrating, and downright unfair.

Let's keep it real – as entrepreneurs of color, women, or veterans, we often find ourselves walking a tightrope when it comes to self-expression. Whether it's rocking a bold hairstyle, wearing clothes that reflect our personality, or just being unapologetically ourselves, we're constantly aware of how we're being perceived. We're judged not just on our skills and ideas, but on how we look, talk, and carry ourselves – and that's not fair.

And let's talk about the double standard when it comes to making mistakes. Minority and women-owned businesses aren't given the same leeway to mess up and learn from it. We're held to a higher standard, expected to be flawless from the get-go. There's no room for trial and error, no grace period to figure things out. It's like we're expected to be perfect from day one, while others are allowed to stumble and grow at their own pace.

And it's not just the outsiders who make it tough for us – sometimes, it's our own people. In a world where opportunities are scarce, it can feel like every success is a threat to someone else's chance to shine. Instead of lifting each other up, we're too busy tearing each other down, judging and criticizing instead of supporting and mentoring.

But here's the thing: despite the obstacles, despite the biases, we're still here. We're still pushing forward, still fighting for our place at the table. "Breaking Barriers" isn't just about airing our grievances – it's about finding solutions. It's about building a community where everyone has a seat, where everyone's voice is heard and valued. here's the thing: I'm here to give you practical advice on how to keep pushing forward, even when the odds are stacked against you.

"Breaking Barriers" isn't just a catchy title – it's a battle cry. It's a reminder that even though the road ahead may be tough, we've got what it takes to conquer it. This chapter is all about arming you with the tools you need to smash through those barriers, to build something incredible in spite of the obstacles in our way. This portion of the book is dedicated to not only highlighting these challenges but also offering real, tangible solutions. We'll share inspiring stories of those who've navigated these waters before, turning obstacles into stepping stones. We're talking about how to build resilience, forge alliances, and create spaces where diversity is not just welcomed but celebrated.

Quick Story Time

Navigating through high school with honors is no small feat, especially when you're bouncing between public and private schools. Imagine stepping into high school; all fired up to dive into a Law program that feels just right, a place where you can finally voice out against the limits clipping your wings. But life, as always, has other plans. The program that once felt like home gets yanked away, and you're tossed among peers who, for reasons unknown, see you as a target rather than a teammate. Maybe it was the freckles, the curves, or just being you in a sea of conformity that set their sights on you. There were so many reasons that I loved this school, but this school did not love me back. It was close to home, and once my brother graduated, things got crazy. All of a sudden, I was a target, accused of looking at other girls' boyfriends, or the boys were looking at me; there was just a multitude of reasons that my family said, enough is enough. They pulled me out of the public school and into the private school where my life was supposed to be different, and all things would be like a fairy tale.

Transitioning to a private school that felt more public than private was a culture shock. The rules were lax, resources scarce, and the small class sizes meant fewer places to hide from the isolation that clung to me tighter with each passing day. Losing my grandfather around this time didn't help. The light inside me dimmed, and the optimistic girl I once knew seemed to fade into the background. It was a strange time, navigating a new educational environment while grappling with grief and the peculiar choice of Christian parents opting for Catholic private schools—a decision that still puzzles me.

But just as I began to find my footing, to make what felt like real connections or what I thought were real connections because the girls didn't like me there either, the rug was pulled from under me again. The school shut down due to financial troubles, and the fragile beginnings of friendships evaporated overnight. It was a harsh lesson in that things are ever-changing, and they don't always last, and the need to get comfortable with being uncomfortable.

Side bar... Have you ever felt like things were going completely crazy in your life, and then all of a sudden, you catch a break? Things began to fall into place, and there is a sense of normalcy, finally. Well, sometimes you are just in the eye of the storm, and if you know anything about being in the eye of the storm, there is really no sign that there is actually a storm going on. The problem with being in the eye of the storm is that you are only in the middle of the "storm", so you are only halfway through, and you need to get through the other half to be out of that storm. Ok, back to the story. Being at this new public/private school was a harsh introduction to the complexities of the world beyond my youthful concerns.

This whirlwind of experiences wasn't just about changing schools or dealing with personal loss; it was a crash course in dealing with being different and the challenges that come with it—both in personal and professional settings. In the business world, much like in those difficult and aggravating school days, being different can be a double-edged sword. It can make you stand out in the best ways, but it can also draw unwarranted jealousy and competition, sometimes even before you've fully found your footing.

In neighborhoods where every achievement feels like a threat to someone else's standing, launching and growing a business becomes a test of resilience. You're not just battling market forces; you're up against a mindset where your success can make you a target. It's a reminder that sometimes, the most significant barriers to our growth are the attitudes and insecurities of those around us.

But here's the thing—being different, whether it's because of how you look, where you come from, or the boldness of your dreams, is your superpower in disguise. It's what sets you apart in a crowded marketplace. The key is to embrace your uniqueness, channel your experiences into your enterprise, and use the lessons learned from every setback as stepping stones to success.

My mom and grandmother found a new private school for me to attend, after the Public Private school closed, and this time, it was an all-girl high school. The classes were still small and similar to other school I attended, but this school was strict. I was just 17, but my boyfriend at the time was 23, a carpenter from whom I learned so much. It was difficult to fit in at this school because I didn't fit in anywhere but here; I was being reprimanded because my hips and butt were too large for my school uniform skirt, and there were no pants that fit me correctly because the size of my waist and hips was not the same and then to be told by my teacher, who I respected while looking at me with her red colored, permed red hair and blue eyes that my reddish blonde hair, that came naturally with my freckled face, needed to be black again because "Black girls aren't born with blonde hair and you must where your natural hair color." I could not have possibly been born with reddish blonde hair, even though I was the most freckled-faced black girl that I knew. I had always been a people-pleaser and rule-abiding young girl, so I tried to do just that. However, my hair turned green and left me at a disadvantage. I was thrown out of Villa Maria that day. My parents sought a lawyer who advised me to show hardship by not attending school for an entire school year; that way, I could sue the school for pain and suffering. I opted out of that because I had already experienced the pain and suffering of leaving behind my peers at three high schools and almost having to dodge bullets from not being "liked" by other girls. I made the decision to go back to my first school, and because I had completed so many credit hours and my grades were really good, I left school every day at 10 am. This allowed me to obtain my first of many jobs.

I know you are thinking, what does this have to do with business and self-help? EVERYTHING!

As we journey through this book together, remember that every challenge and roadblock is just another chapter in your story of triumph. Let's use this space, this shared experience, to learn, grow, and build businesses that reflect our most authentic selves, freckles, hips, and all. Let's elevate on this…

Think about the challenges you're facing right now. Do any of them remind you of obstacles you encountered in your childhood?

Maybe it's the feeling of being underestimated or overlooked, or perhaps it's the struggle to be taken seriously in certain spaces. Whatever it is, let's dig deeper into these parallels.

For example, remember those times when you felt like you had to shrink yourself to fit into other people's expectations? Maybe you were told to tone down your personality or conform to a certain image to be accepted. Well, guess what? Those same pressures might be showing up in your business journey today. Maybe you're hesitant to fully express your creativity or embrace your unique style because you're worried about how others will perceive you. Sound familiar?

Or how about those moments when you had to fight twice as hard for recognition or opportunities simply because of who you are? Maybe you were overlooked for leadership roles or passed over for certain opportunities because you didn't fit the mold of what a "successful" person looked like. Well, those same biases and barriers might be holding you back in your entrepreneurial pursuits today.

But here's the thing – just like you did back then, you have the power to overcome these obstacles. You have the resilience, the creativity, and the determination to push through and carve out your own path. So, let's lean into these parallels, let's reflect on the lessons we learned from our childhood challenges, and let's use them to fuel our journey toward success.

Remember, every obstacle is just another opportunity to prove how strong and capable you truly are. So, embrace your journey, embrace your authenticity, and let's continue to rise above the challenges together.

Embracing Uniqueness in a Uniform World

The challenges I faced in trying to conform to the strict standards of an all-girls private school, from the issues with my uniform fitting my body type to the criticism over my natural hair color, highlight a reality many minority and women-owned businesses face: the pressure to conform to traditional norms and expectations. In business, this pressure can manifest in how we brand ourselves, the products or services we offer, and even in the way we communicate with our market. The lesson here is about the strength found in embracing our uniqueness. It's about understanding that being different isn't a disadvantage; it's a distinct competitive edge.

The Power of Racism and Bias

The comment about my hair color—"Black girls aren't born with blonde hair"—is a stark reminder of the biases and racism that permeate not just educational institutions but the business world as well. Minority and women-owned businesses often face systemic barriers, from difficulty accessing loans and capital to biases in contract awards and networking opportunities. While these challenges are real, acknowledging them is the first step toward overcoming them. Statistics have shown that businesses owned by women and minorities are growing, but they still face significant hurdles in reaching the same level of success as their counterparts.

Favor and Resiliency

Choosing not to pursue legal action against the school and instead returning to my original high school was a decision rooted in looking forward, not backward. It's about picking your battles and knowing when to focus your energies on building rather than battling. This mindset is crucial in business. There will be setbacks and injustices, but the ability to persevere, to find favor even in less-than-ideal circumstances, and to keep pushing forward is what sets successful entrepreneurs apart. It's not just about surviving; it's about thriving despite the odds.

Perseverance in Business

My early departure from school each day led me to my first job, an opportunity that wouldn't have been available if I hadn't faced and overcome the challenges before. This speaks volumes about the importance of perseverance. In the context of business, perseverance might mean pushing through rejection, navigating financial struggles, or continuing to innovate in the face of failure. Remember, every successful business owner has faced challenges; it's how they respond to these challenges that define their path.

Unpacking Trauma and Moving Forward

Understanding and unpacking the trauma from these experiences is not just about healing; it's about gathering the strength and wisdom to move forward. In business, this means taking the lessons learned from every setback and using them to build a stronger, more resilient foundation for your future endeavors. It's about knowing that favor doesn't come from fitting in; it comes from standing out, from being authentically yourself in a world that often tells you otherwise.

My journey through different schools, facing bias, and learning to navigate through a world that didn't always accept me mirrors the entrepreneurial journey. It's filled with ups and downs, but at its core, it's a story of resilience, of finding favor in adversity, and of the undeniable power of perseverance. Let's take these lessons and apply them to our businesses, to our personal growth, and to the way we move through the world. Together, we can turn our trials into triumphs, using every challenge as a stepping stone to greater success.

Here are some lessons that I learned about myself throughout these situations, now that I'm on the outside looking in.

Navigating through life's transitions and challenges, especially when they hit us back-to-back, teaches us invaluable lessons that are directly applicable to both our personal growth and our business ventures. Let's break down these experiences into tangible lessons and takeaways that can guide us on our journey:

Lesson 1: Understanding the Impact of Transitions
Key Takeaway: Transitions, especially after a significant loss, can profoundly affect us. It's like trying to find your footing when the ground beneath you keeps shifting. This isn't just a personal issue; it spills over into every aspect of life, including business. When we're in the middle of a transition, whether it's moving to a new city, changing schools, or even starting a new business venture, it's crucial to recognize the potential for emotional turmoil, such as depression. The lesson here is to be gentle with ourselves during these times and seek support when needed. Our businesses, much like us, feel the ripple effects of our emotional state, so staying mindful and proactive about our mental health is key.

Lesson 2: Recognizing Isolation as a Sign of Trauma
Key Takeaway: Isolation is a common response to trauma. It's like hiding away and secretly licking our wounds away from prying eyes. While it might feel like a protective measure, isolating ourselves can prevent us from receiving the support and help we need. In business, this can translate to withdrawing from networking opportunities, hesitating to ask for help, or even ignoring valuable feedback. Recognizing isolation as a coping mechanism allows us to consciously choose more constructive ways to heal and grow, both personally and professionally.

Lesson 3: The Illusion of the Grass Being Greener
Key Takeaway: Just because something looks better on the surface doesn't mean it truly is. My transition from a

free inner-city school to a "better" private school, which promised a "superior education" but instead delivered a traumatic experience, serves as a powerful metaphor. In business, this translates to being lured in by others with the idea of seemingly lucrative opportunities that may not align with our values or may come with hidden costs. The lesson is to do *our due diligence*, look beyond the surface, and to make informed decisions. Protect your business like you would protect a child, with careful consideration and a healthy dose of skepticism. Preparation for potential biases and discriminatory practices is also crucial; understanding how to navigate these challenges with grace and resilience can make all the difference in both personal and professional arenas.

Integrating Lessons Into Life and Business:

These experiences, though tough, equip us with a unique set of skills and insights. They teach us the importance of resilience, the value of support systems, and the power of informed decision-making. As we navigate the complexities of life and business, let's use these lessons as a compass, guiding us through the challenges and toward our goals with wisdom, courage, and a deep understanding of our own strength and resilience. Remember, every challenge is an opportunity to learn, grow, and emerge stronger on the other side.

Let's look at some tangible solutions and Inspirational Stories

Let's dive into these stories of resilience and innovation, where entrepreneurs have faced down adversity and come out on top. From navigating through the toughest of times to finding innovative solutions, their journeys offer invaluable lessons for us all.

Through these tales, we'll uncover practical strategies for building up resilience, forming powerful alliances, and fostering diversity in our own entrepreneurial pursuits. It's not just about facing the challenges – it's about turning them into opportunities for growth and success.

So, buckle up and get ready to be inspired. Together, we'll explore the paths of those who've triumphed over adversity, and we'll discover how to carve out our own paths to success in the face of bias and racism.

Story of Resilience: Madam C.J. Walker
Madam C.J. Walker, born Sarah Breedlove, was the first female self-made millionaire in America, a monumental achievement for an African American woman at the turn of the 20th century. Facing racial and gender biases, Madam Walker created a line of hair care products specifically for Black women, addressing a market need while empowering her community.

Lesson Learned: Find a niche where you can make a significant impact. Madam Walker's success teaches us the importance of identifying unmet needs within your community and using your unique position to address them. It's about turning what makes you different into your biggest asset.

Story of Innovation: Arlan Hamilton
Arlan Hamilton, a Black, gay woman, founded Backstage Capital, a venture capital fund dedicated to minimizing funding disparities in tech by investing in high-potential

startups led by underrepresented founders. Starting from homelessness, Hamilton broke into the VC world, a space notoriously difficult for minorities and women to penetrate.

Lesson Learned: Use your perspective to innovate within existing structures. Hamilton's journey underscores the importance of persistence and the willingness to challenge the status quo. For entrepreneurs facing bias, remember that your unique viewpoint is invaluable and capable of uncovering opportunities others might overlook.

Story of Unity: WeWork Veterans In Residence Program
The WeWork Veterans In Residence Program, powered by Bunker Labs, is a national initiative offering workspace, services, and community to help veteran entrepreneurs build and grow their businesses. This program exemplifies how creating alliances can provide the necessary support and resources to overcome systemic barriers.

Lesson Learned: Seek out or create supportive communities and alliances. For service-disabled veterans and others facing obstacles in business, finding or establishing networks can offer both practical resources and the emotional support needed to navigate entrepreneurship's challenges.

When we are speaking, teaching and empowering our younger and/ or less experienced counterparts here a few things that we need to do to assure that we create the space and set the tone for those who are coming after us.

Celebrate Success Stories: Regularly highlight and celebrate the achievements of minority, women, and veteran entrepreneurs within our communities. This not only provides role models but also shifts the narrative towards a more inclusive and diverse representation of success

Foster Inclusive Networks: Build or participate in networks that actively include and support diverse entrepreneurs. These can be local business groups, online communities, or industry-specific associations that prioritize diversity and inclusion.

Offer Mentorship and Resources: Establish mentorship programs that connect experienced entrepreneurs with those just starting, focusing on overcoming the unique challenges faced by underrepresented groups. Additionally, create or share resources that address specific needs, such as access to funding, navigating discrimination, or building resilience.

Encourage Open Dialogue: Promote discussions about bias, racism, and diversity in your business and community. Open dialogue can educate, raise awareness, and foster a more supportive environment for everyone.

Overcoming bias and racism in business isn't just about individual resilience; it's about collective action, innovation, and creating spaces where diversity isn't just tolerated but celebrated. By drawing inspiration from those who've paved the way, seeking supportive communities, and advocating for diversity, entrepreneurs can turn obstacles into opportunities for growth and change.

Before you move into the next chapter, I want to make a disclaimer that I am in no way, shape or form trying to change anyone's mind on where they are with God or telling them what to do. Please remember that this is my book and my experiences that I am using to explain the things that I've gone through and to assist you, by being transparent. If you are triggered by the next chapter, read it ANYWAY! Business is not about "Feeling" good. Sometimes, we are forced to deal with things that we are uncomfortable dealing with. You know what's uncomfortable? Being BROKE is uncomfortable, and so is being BROKEN. Let's be sure to be honest about how we feel and move forward, facing the adversity and having the hard conversations. Grab your pen, and let's dive in.

Chapter 4:

Breaking Chains: Overcoming Business Restrictions to Unlock Growth and Empowerment

Problem: Restrictions placed on us could negatively affect the way we think and how quickly we take action in our business and in our personal lives. When it feels like there are barriers all around us, it's not just about the physical hurdles we have to jump over. These restrictions, the ones that seem to be holding us back, can really mess with our heads. They start to shape the way we think, making us doubt our moves and slow down our steps, both in our businesses and in our day-to-day lives.

Imagine you're ready to sprint, full speed ahead, toward your business goals or personal dreams. But then, you notice these hurdles—rules that don't make sense, people doubting your ability because of where you come from, your shape, size or the color of your skin, or even just the inner voice telling you it's not possible. These are the restrictions we're talking about. They're like invisible chains that can hold us back from moving as fast and freely as we want.

But here's the deal: knowing about these barriers is the first step to breaking them down. It's about understanding that these challenges are real, but they don't define what we can achieve. We've got to switch up our mindset to start seeing these hurdles not as stop signs but as stepping stones. It's time to push back against those doubts, to take action with confidence, and to move forward with the knowledge that we can overcome anything thrown our way.

So, as we dive into this journey together, let's keep it real with ourselves. Let's acknowledge the restrictions but refuse to let them dictate our pace. It's all about breaking those chains, one step at a time, and moving towards our goals with determination and resilience.

As soon as we saw the word RESTRICTED, we immediately began to tense up. Did you see your face when you saw that RE?! When I say, you were about to close the book, I felt that in my energy, and you better not because that is exactly what that world wants us to do: QUIT! The word Business alone tends to scare people, and others throw it around to make other people feel bad, like "Girl, I'm a whole "Business Owner" when they aren't half of anything the whole time, but that's another story. Stay focused; I was starting to drift, Lol. You know me, friend. The word Restrictive means to impose limitations on someone's activities or freedom. Seriously, there are so many RESTRICTIONS it makes my head hurt even writing it out, so from now on, instead of writing the word "RESTRICT", I'm gonna call it "IT". If you are a religious person and you are reading this book, you may want to skim through this chapter because I'm going to talk a little bit about us and the "ITS" that are placed on us because we LOVE GOD!

Church "ITS"
Christian living can be "IT"ive. Did y'all catch how I wrote that out? It wasn't a typo. Remember a couple of sentences ago, we agreed that I was no longer going to use

that "R" word and instead, I would use "IT" and its place, so I'll leave you to figure that out (Sidebar)

There are so many expectations placed on us, especially women in business and what we should and should not do when it comes to this beautiful word called Business that sometimes all of the "ITS" cause us to want to quit the startup portion of our business or just our business altogether whether established or on the way to being established. It's bad enough that most of us, black men and women, come from ritualistic churches comprised of ritualistic services, which are process-based, repeatable and symbolic actions that occur during service. There is absolutely nothing wrong with this, and this is the very foundation that we have been built on, but God is the big G.O.D., and we need to treat God accordingly. The "ITS", similar to today's society, causes isolation and separation between God and business when, in actuality, business comes from God. The teachings and strategy of Business comes from our very strategic G.O.D., but that's for another day and time and will be highlighted in volume 2, PERIOD! There are a few things I want to address, specifically the type of church that I grew up in and its expectation versus reality" of living a Christian life while pursuing entrepreneurship. Growing up in the church, I was taught to lead with faith, to believe in the power of prayer, and to always put God first in all my endeavors. This foundation has been crucial in my journey, but it also presented unique challenges, especially as a woman in business. The church often emphasizes humility, patience, and trust in God's timing, which are all virtuous qualities. However, in the fast-paced world of business, these teachings sometimes seem at odds with the aggressive, assertive posture often required to succeed. These contrasting ideas can leave us feeling torn, as if we must choose between our spiritual values and the demands of our business ventures. Yet, I've come to understand that this perceived conflict is a false. God's teachings are not only compatible with business success; they are foundational to it. The principles of stewardship, integrity, service, and love are not just spiritual ideals; they are also the hallmarks of sustainable, meaningful business practices.

For women and minorities in business, especially those of us from church backgrounds, there's an added layer of complexity. We navigate not just the challenges of entrepreneurship but also the systemic barriers and biases that can make our paths even more difficult. It's here, in these challenges, that our faith can be our greatest asset. Faith gives us resilience, a sense of purpose, and a community to lean on for support, advice, and encouragement. So, to my fellow entrepreneurs from the church, I say this: Your faith is not a hindrance to your business success; it is your secret weapon. The values you've been raised with, the community that supports you, and your belief in something greater than yourself - these are all powerful drivers of ethical, impactful business practices. Embrace them. Let them guide you not just in your personal life but in your business dealings as well. As we continue to break barriers and build our businesses, let us not forget where we come from. Let us use our platforms to not only generate wealth but also to create positive change, uplift our communities, and reflect the teachings of our faith in every decision we make. In doing so, we bridge the gap between God and business, showing the world that it's not just about success; it's about significance. And remember, when the going gets tough, and the "ITS" seem too much to bear, lean into your faith, your community, and the teachings that have brought you this far. In the intersection of faith and entrepreneurship, there's a unique space for us to redefine success on our terms, rooted in our values and uplifted by our beliefs.

So, let's continue to navigate this journey with grace, tenacity, and the unwavering belief that with God, all things are possible, not just in church but in the boardroom, the marketplace, and beyond. Let's make our mark, driven by faith, and lead by example, showing that Christian living can indeed be "IT"ive in every aspect of our lives, including business. Let's unpack some of the things that happen to us in our churches and how they should be addressed, but until then, how should we navigate them?

1. **Addressing the guilt around attendance,** let's dive deep into this because it's a shared experience for all of us church-going business owners. The subtle jabs, the disapproving glances, and even those direct but funny accusations from the pulpit questioning our commitment because we're not present at every single service. *Let's be clear: this needs to stop.* This kind of pressure doesn't just create a divide; it leaves a sour taste and silently discourages us from inviting others into our church community. *Why?* Because deep down, some of us are contemplating leaving, h*eld back only by fear.* **Yes, I've said it loud and clear**. If that truth hits hard and makes you want to close this book or even shout from the rooftops,

know that you're not alone. These imposed "ITS" have stifled our voices, *but no more*. You feel that thing in the bottom of your stomach or your throat, and you want to address it, but that just doesn't seem right because the "ITS" that have been placed on you MAKE YOU HAVE RESTRAINT and STOP YOU FROM SPEAKING OUT! I've been through enough prayer and fasting to live freely and share this message, sanctioned by the Almighty Himself. Reflecting on James 2:12, *"Speak and act as those who are going to be judged by the law that gives us freedom,"* reminds us that we're all equal under God's grace, freed from the shackles of judgment and sin.

2. **Making everything about money.** Let's talk about the fixation of money within the church walls. I can speak for myself and share a small story. When my business began to grow, and I was a young woman who attended church every Sunday unless I was extremely sick, I struggled with balance horribly. I heard the sly comments, I saw the twisted-up faces, and I felt the pressure and the "ITS." It was as if my business was made small, and the church needed to be number 1, so I would try and give as much as I could because I was unable to be in attendance. I have to be honest and say that it worked for a minute. I gave money when I really didn't have it to give, but I gave it anyway. There was no one there to teach me about my finances. No one talked to me about investments. Instead, it was always about what I could give, not what would be given to me. I've employed people at my church, and that still wasn't enough to lift the heaviness of the judgment and "ITS" I was dealing with. I had to make up in my mind that I was going to practice financial health, no matter what anyone

else said or thought and I'd began to invest my money in my business and my not-for-profit, regardless of outside opinions.

3. **Using people.** Lastly, the issue of exploitation within our churches cannot go unmentioned. It's a delicate subject, but it's crucial to address. The expectation for members to offer their professional services for free is not just unfair—it's demeaning. This practice risks burnout and imposes undue burdens. Instead, our churches should nurture talents, maybe through business education or transforming into hubs of enterprise as they once were. Imagine a community where services and skills are exchanged, not demanded—a place where volunteerism within businesses is encouraged as a form of barter. These ideas aren't just whims; they're essential discussions for fostering a supportive, thriving church community that values contribution without exploitation.

In weaving these narratives into our broader story, it's clear that the path forward involves respect, understanding, and mutual support. By addressing these "ITS" head-on, we can build a church community that not only respects but champions the entrepreneurial spirit, aligning our spiritual journey with our business ambitions. It's about creating a space where faith and enterprise coexist harmoniously, supporting each other in a cycle of growth, generosity, and grace.

Society "ITS"
Aside from all of the other "ITS" we have, here comes good ole Society. You will be "IT'ED" based on so many different things. The reason Society's ITS can be so difficult to

overcome is that the people who are placing the ITS on us are no longer limited to our small inner circle like they tend to be in Church. Having to fight against your "OWN" group of people is one thing because at least you know that with your own people, there is always space for you. When you are dealing with the "ITS" of Society, the isolation can be real and very substantial. In Society, you are no longer able to just BLEND in like you've been trying to do your whole life. Who you are will bleed through your clothes like a heavy menstrual and seep out of your pores like the smell of an alcoholic who has promised you that they are no longer drinking, but they've had a drink on the way over. Take this time and reflect while you read through these" IT'S". *Disclaimer* This may be the time that you refill your glass of punch, wine, coffee, etc... It's about to get a little deep. These three (Society IT'S) are what each and every one of us has experienced at some point in our lives.

1. **Judging Others because of their socio-economic status.** Socioeconomic status is the position of an individual or group on the socioeconomic scale, which is determined by a combination of social and economic factors such as income, amount and kind of education, type and prestige of occupation, place of residence, ethnic origin or religious background. This simply means that who you were raised by and what neighborhood you grew up in can define how Society treats you. It can be the color of your skin, the style of clothing you wear, the neighborhood you grew up in, who your parents are and even what kind of vehicle you drive or if you drive one at all. We have so many things that can "IT" us.

2. **Grouping individuals together.** Society says that because of point number one, I'm going to assume that people who live in a certain neighborhood are bad people. I'm going to assume that people who listen to a certain type of music are the same. Society once told us that women were inferior to men. Society depicted that women were to be home makers. That our place was in the home, accepting whatever a man brought to us, and that was it. If your husband wanted Children, then it was your job, your duty, to have children. If, for whatever reason, you were unable to bear children, you were considered even more inferior, and you were depicted as worthless. This stigma has somewhat changed over time but has not stopped those with the inability or the lack of desire to change from re-assuring us women that we must stay in our proper place. Society can be tough on us, making us feel judged for all sorts of reasons that go way beyond our friends and family. This kind of judgment can make us feel really alone and like we're constantly being tested. It's not just about small disagreements; it's about feeling like you're being pushed away because of who you are. Sometimes, if you don't have a lot or if you come from a certain place, people might treat you like you're not worth as much or you can't do great things. This kind of judgment can happen in sneaky ways, like when someone is surprised you're smart or good at something because of where you're from. Or it can be really obvious, like not getting a job or a place to live because of these things. It's like people put you in a box based on what you have or don't have, and they forget about what you can do or who you really are.

Trying to be true to yourself when society wants you to fit in can be really hard. There's a lot of pressure to act a certain way or hide what makes you unique. This can be even harder for people who are trying to start their own business, especially if they're women or come from a minority group. They have to deal with all the normal challenges of starting a business, plus extra pressure from society's judgments.

We need to make places where everyone can be themselves and share their stories without being judged. This starts with us questioning what we think is "*normal*" or "*right*" and appreciating the different ways people live their lives. Let's work towards building a world where we support each other instead of judging. We need to be brave and kind and believe that we can make things better. By understanding each other and breaking down the walls that society has built, we can create a future where everyone has the chance to be who they are and achieve their dreams without being held back by old-fashioned ideas.

Self "ITS"
We can be our own worst critic. We can be "IT" in our own lives. We place limits on ourselves for many different reasons, causing further damage than previously experienced.

The one thing that we cannot stand is looking at and dealing with the *"Person in the Mirror"*. See, we can doll ourselves up and stare at how beautiful we look in the reflection of the mirror, but we don't want to spend time combing through the issues of the person standing in front of the reflection. Think about the last time you were in your bathroom, and you were standing there at the sink, brushing your teeth, washing your face, putting on your makeup or styling your hair. While you are focusing on whichever activity, you may be thinking about what your boss said last week or what your boyfriend said yesterday that caused you to go back and change your outfit before the big event. The next thing you know, you are in that same mirror, talking to yourself. That mirror has now become your go-to girl. What started out as the uncomfortable "mirror time" has become your best friend, but only in that moment. Only if we saw ourselves as our friends see us, maybe then we'd be kinder to ourselves.

As business owners, especially those of us who are minorities and women, we often face a double challenge. Not only do we have to deal with all the usual difficulties of running a business, but we also face extra barriers because of who we are. These barriers aren't just physical; they're in our heads, too. We doubt ourselves, question our abilities, and sometimes, we even think that we don't deserve success. This kind of thinking is what I call the "Self ITS," where we become our own roadblocks.

Why do we do this to ourselves? A lot of it comes from the messages we've heard all of our lives. Maybe people told us we couldn't succeed because of our background, our gender, or the color of our skin. Over time, we start to believe these messages, even if they're not true. And these beliefs can lead us to treat ourselves, and sometimes even others, unfairly. We might push people away, doubt their intentions, or become overly critical, mirroring the very attitudes we despise.

But here's the thing: the person in the mirror—your *"go-to girl"* or *guy*—is also your biggest cheerleader. That reflection is someone who's overcome obstacles, who keeps pushing forward, and who deserves every bit of success that comes their way. It's time to start recognizing that person's worth.

How do we change this? How do we remove these "Self ITS" and stop the cycle of doubt and self-criticism?

1. **Talk to yourself like you would to a friend**: Would you tell your friend they're not good enough because of where they come from or because they're a woman or a minority? Of course not. So, why say those things to yourself? Start by being kinder in your self-talk.

2. **Celebrate your achievements:** No matter how small they may seem, every win is a step forward. Celebrating your successes helps build confidence and breaks down those mental barriers.

3. **Seek support:** Surround yourself with people who believe in you and your vision. This can be a formal network of other business owners or just friends and family who want to see you succeed.

4. **Educate yourself:** Knowledge is power. The more you know about your business and your industry, the more confident you'll feel. And confidence is key to overcoming self-doubt.

5. **Take care of yourself:** Running a business is hard work, but you can't do it if you're running on empty. Make sure to take time for yourself, whether it's reading a book, going

for a walk, or just taking a few moments each day to breathe and reflect.

Remember, the person in the mirror has gotten you this far. They have the strength, the intelligence, and the resilience to go even further. It's time to start believing in them.

In the mirror is where you are safe. You are talking to yourself, and you know yourself better than anyone else, so that is a safe space.

STORY TIME:

Let's dig into a chat as deep and flavorful as the journey of some of our most legendary entrepreneurs. Today, we're shining a spotlight on none other than Martha Stewart – a name that sparks more than just thoughts of recipes and home decor. Martha's story is gripping, not just for the drama it stirred up, but for the epic comeback that followed. **Now, let me be real upfront: breaking the law is not cool.** But Martha's journey from controversy to kicking butt again teaches us a thing or two about bouncing back, reinventing, and hustling hard to reclaim success.

Martha Stewart's tale is not just about the fall; it's about the epic rise that came after. After doing her time, Martha didn't just bounce back to where she was before; she rebuilt and expanded her empire, becoming even more of a boss in the process. It shows that setbacks, no matter how rough, are not the end of the story – they're just a bump in the road.

So why am I bringing up Martha's saga? 'Cause it shines a light on a bigger issue: the uneven playing field in the business world, especially for women and minorities. When Martha faced the heat and got convicted, it raised serious questions about fairness and bias in how folks are judged and punished in the business game. But it also proves a powerful point: resilience and innovation can bust through barriers, even when the world has its eyes on you.

Now, let's switch gears to some seriously inspiring tales of minority and women-owned businesses crushing it. Check out Lisa Price, for example. She turned her kitchen experiments into the mega-successful beauty brand Carol's Daughter. Her story, just like Martha's, is all about turning what some might see as negatives into major positives. They found their niches, often in spots others overlooked, and built empires by meeting needs that folks weren't paying attention to before.

What these stories teach us is that barriers and haters, while tough, are not unbeatable. Lisa Price took her love for natural beauty and turned it into a brand that celebrates the authenticity and diversity of beauty across cultures. She, like Martha, faced hurdles and critics but came out on top by staying true to their vision and never giving up.

So, as we chew on these stories, let's remember that the path to success isn't always smooth sailing. It's full of bumps, detours, and maybe even some dead ends. But it's also brimming with chances to grow, change course, and come out on top. Whether you're in the kitchen, the boardroom, or anywhere in between, your potential to make waves is limitless. Let these stories fuel your fire to find your groove, embrace your strengths, and carve out your own success story, no matter what gets in your way. Because remember, it ain't about where you start; it's about where you're headed and how you hustle to get there.

I've been working in the construction industry for over 15 years, a job area where you see a lot more men than women. I don't just work here; I run my own company that does everything in construction, and I help manage big building projects for my city's Industrial Development Agency. In this time, I've seen a lot of unfair treatment because I'm a woman and because of my race. People often talk about how today's world is more open, saying that as a woman, I should feel free to speak up about any unfair treatment I face. But—and it's a big "but"—even though they say I can talk about these problems, I also have to be ready for some people to push back or treat me even worse for speaking up. The society acts like it's got my back, but really, it feels like there's only so much protection it will give

In my job, I've had to deal with some pretty tough stuff. There's been a lot of disrespect, where people think I can't be as good because I'm a woman, or they treat me differently because of my race. It's like there's an unspoken rule that I'm supposed to stay quiet and just put up with it. But here's the thing: I've learned that speaking up is important, even if it's scary and even if some people might not like it. Because every time I do, I'm not just standing up for myself; I'm standing up for everyone who's been treated unfairly in jobs like mine.

But let me tell you, it's not all bad. Yes, I've faced some really tough times, but I've also met some amazing people along the way. There are others in construction who believe in fairness and respect, and we've got each other's backs. Together, we're slowly but surely making changes, showing that it doesn't matter if you're a woman or what your race is—you can do the job and do it well.

So, what's my message to anyone reading this? Even though society might say one thing and do another, don't let that stop you. If you're facing unfair treatment, talk about it. Find people who will support you. And never forget that you deserve to be treated with respect and fairness, no matter what job you're doing. It's not easy, I won't lie. But it's worth it because every small step we take is one step closer to making our workplaces—and our world—a better place for everyone.

Chapter 5:

Rising Strong: Turning Adversity into Triumph

In this chapter, we're getting real about facing the toughest of challenges head-on, with a spotlight on the journey of a young single mama navigating through some rough waters of domestic violence. It's all about taking the struggles we've faced and turning them into lessons of strength, resilience, and ultimate victory. Through raw, true-to-life stories and down-to-earth advice, we're diving deep into how to break free from the cycles of abuse, rebuild our sense of self-worth, and set the stage for a future filled with empowerment and triumph. Consider this chapter your roadmap for navigating through the darkest of times, offering a guiding light, a glimmer of hope, and some practical steps to help you pave your own path toward a brighter, more empowered future.

The ABUSIVE RELATIONSHIP

I grew up seeing so many different things, and I had experienced entrepreneurship or business ownership at a young age, but responsibility hit me hard. By 19, I was a mother and in and out of an abusive relationship. Life was really "lifing" me. Because I was no longer living at home and I was a college drop-out, the reality that no one was coming to save me kicked in. I began searching for that child-like faith I had in my past. I was still, technically, a teenager, and I had family who loved me, but we all know that once you are out of your parent's house and you experience freedom, you do not want to go back. Besides being physically abused or physically fighting, the mental abuse was far stronger than I really knew. I had come to a place where I no longer liked what I saw in the mirror.

At this point, you may be asking yourself why I'm sharing things like this in a self-help book, and the answer is simple because a lot of others don't tell the REAL story, the WHOLE story. We want to discuss how we "WOKE UP LIKE THIS", and that is not the truth in any of our stories. It is necessary to explain the traumas so you can realize that you can achieve ANYTHING no matter what you've been through.

The trauma was real, and it had nothing to do with the man; it had everything to do with me and where I was. I never stopped going to church. I attended Bible Study regularly and even sang in the choir, but did anyone see me? My dad was still running his business and, so I knew I could go to him, but I refused. Every time I attempted to pick myself up and move forward, something would happen. I needed to leave this man behind, and in my mind, all I needed was a car to get myself and my baby around, and then I could leave for sure. So, I purchased a vehicle with my school refund check; I was enrolled in Cosmetology School, but anyway, on St. Patrick's Day weekend, while waiting to take my full coverage photos for Monday, my car was smashed to smithereens by a drunk driver who kept going. I heard the hit; the impact was horrendous, and I felt it in my gut. Not only had I just lost my grandmother a couple of weeks before, but now I had lost my ticket out of this abusive relationship. Our bed was a mattress on the floor in the building that my dad owned. No one was invited to our apartment because we were undone, and they had no idea that if he got upset, he would padlock me in the house with the baby. I didn't even have a cellphone because that was not in our budget. My life was ruined. The encouragement I gave myself was that it'll just be a little longer. *He wasn't a bad guy every day*, and *he didn't get upset for no reason*; I *knew how to deal with him*, and *I was not in a "Real" abusive situation. We just fought sometimes*. These are things I told myself daily, so much so that I began to believe them. It was a life far from what I had envisioned for myself.

Why share such pain in a book aimed at guiding others in business and personal growth? Because it's crucial to acknowledge where we've been to understand how far we've come. This story isn't just about abuse or loss; it's about the lies we tell ourselves to cope and the truths we must face to move forward. I told myself it wasn't *"real" abuse* and that we were just two people who fought too much, but deep down, I knew I deserved better and that my child deserved better.

The journey from that point to where I am now wasn't easy. It required confronting harsh realities, making tough decisions, and slowly rebuilding my sense of self-worth. But it was possible. And that's the message I want to impart: no matter the depths of despair, change is within reach. You are not defined by your current circumstances but by your ability to rise above them.

For anyone reading this who sees a reflection of their own struggles in my story, know that your current situation is not your final destination. The road to overcoming is paved with small, often difficult steps toward self-love, empowerment, and, eventually, freedom. The business of rebuilding starts with believing you are worthy of a life filled with respect, love, and success. Let this chapter be a reminder that resilience is born from adversity and that every day offers a new opportunity to choose a different path. The trauma was real, and AGAIN, it had nothing to do with the man; it had everything to do with me and where I was. I say this to say that we MUST stop blaming others for what we accept!

The journey from adversity to empowerment, as illustrated through personal struggles such as overcoming an abusive relationship and the challenges of single motherhood, offers profound insights for minority, women, and veteran-owned businesses. Here are some key takeaways that resonate deeply with the entrepreneurial spirit and the unique hurdles faced by these groups:

1. **Be Strong, Bounce Back:** Resilience is your secret weapon. Just like how you pick yourself up after personal struggles, in business, especially as a minority, woman, or veteran, resilience is what keeps you going. No matter how many times life knocks you down with rejection or bias, you've got the strength to rise again.

2. **Build Your Squad:** Just like you lean on your friends and family in tough times, in business, having a support network is key. Find mentors, join business groups, and connect with folks who've walked similar paths. These networks aren't just about practical advice; they're about having folks who get it and got your back

3. **Take Charge of Your Destiny:** Entrepreneurship is your ticket to freedom and empowerment. It's like breaking free from a toxic relationship – it puts you in control of your future, letting you build something meaningful on your own terms. For those who've felt powerless, owning a business is a way to reclaim your power and make a positive impact.

4. **Show 'Em What You're Made Of:** Dealing with bias ain't easy, but excellence speaks louder than prejudice. By showing up with top-notch work and integrity, you break down stereotypes and prove your worth. It's about letting your success do the talking and shaking up the status quo.

5. **Believe in Yourself:** Self-doubt can be a real stagnating, but confidence is key. Especially for minority, women and veteran entrepreneurs, who face doubters at every turn, believing in yourself is non-negotiable. Build up that self-worth and shut down the haters.

6. **Turn Pain into Power:** Just like personal struggles can lead to growth, business challenges can spark innovation. They show you new paths, new markets, and help you connect with customers on a deeper level. Embrace your story, scars and all, and watch how it resonates with others.

7. **Be the Change:** Speaking out about personal experiences creates awareness, and advocating for diversity and inclusion in business can spark real change. As minority, women, and veteran entrepreneurs, you've got the power to lead by

example and push for a more inclusive world. You may be the only one in your family to go to college or you may be a teenage mom who feels like your life is over and I'm here to tell you that YOU CAN CHANGE THE NARRATIVE! You are the author of the book that you choose to write for you and your child(ren).

Chapter 6:

From the Ground Up Embracing the Multifaceted Path to Self-Mastery"

In "From the Ground Up," we delve deep into the foundational experiences that shape not just a business but the entrepreneur behind it. "From the Ground Up" is all about the real deal of starting your own thing, your own hustle, from scratch.

Picture this: you're down in a basement. Maybe it's your family's, or maybe it's just a spot you found where you can get to work. This isn't just any room; it's where you're planting the seeds for your future business, even if it doesn't feel like it yet. It's just you, your ideas, and maybe a bit of frustration because, let's be real, starting something new is tough.

This chapter dives into those early days when you're trying to figure it all out. *You're handling money with a tight budget, trying to sell something when you've never sold anything in your life, and facing challenge after challenge.* **That basement?** It's more than a place; it's a symbol of starting from the bottom, of building something significant from very little.

Now, let's elevate about the rollercoaster of emotions that comes with this territory. There's gonna be moments when you're mad, when you're feeling stuck and when you wonder if it's all worth it. These feelings are like unexpected teachers. They school you into being tough, switching up your game when needed, and finding strength you didn't even know you had. Especially for us in the Black community, we're often working with less—**less money, less support** and **fewer chances**. But that doesn't mean we can't make it. It means we've got to be smarter, more resilient, and ready to face those extra hurdles head-on.

But here's the kicker: those tough times aren't just problems; they're your path to getting better. They teach you every single thing you need to know about running your business. It's about taking ownership and really getting the feel of your hustle inside and out. This kind of knowledge? Baby, listen! You can't just read about it; you've got to live it. It shapes you into, not just a boss, but a leader who gets what everyone's going through because you've been there, too.

"From the Ground Up" isn't just storytelling. It's about hitting you with the truth that every big win starts with small steps. It's a call to keep pushing, to rely on yourself, and to be cool with wearing different hats because each one teaches you something new. This chapter is here to light that fire, to show you that where you begin doesn't define where you'll end up. It's a shout-out to remember that greatness can, and often does, start from the ground up.

So, as you flip through these pages, see them as a reflection of your own grind and a glimpse into what's possible. It's a reminder that greatness has humble beginnings, and yeah, it can rise right from the ground up.

This chapter centers around the transformative journey from frustration to enlightenment, beginning in the humble confines of a basement. It's here, amid the solitude and shadows, where the seeds of entrepreneurship are unwillingly sown by necessity and nurtured by the relentless drive for something more.

However, as the narrative unfolds, so does the realization that these early trials are not merely obstacles but opportunities. They are chances to learn every aspect of running a business from the ground up, instilling a sense of ownership and a depth of understanding that cannot be taught, but **MUST** be experienced.

The BASEMENT

Despite my myriad of jobs—from collection agencies to banks and dental offices—nothing stuck. I was searching for something more, a purpose that resonated with my soul, even though I didn't quite know what that was yet. At 22, after floating through life on the breeze of temporary jobs and fleeting relationships, my dad's call for help felt like an anchor thrown my way. Little did I know, this anchor would eventually ground me in ways I never imagined.

In the early chapters of my life, working in my dad's plumbing company was the last place I thought I'd find my calling.

I was a daddy's girl and I loved my daddy with all of my heart, but I did not want to work in a dirty plumbing company. It wasn't just about the dirt and grime associated with plumbing; it was about carving my own path, separate from the legacy my father built. My father didn't really know me. He didn't know the knowledge that I had because he was too busy trailblazing the way for me. He and I were like trains in the night just passing by in the weekends and tha had come to an end, I was a WHOLE ENTIRE WOMAN! By this point, I had been to cosmetology school and worked in and out of some salons. The money in the hair industry was quick and easy, like selling drugs, but it didn't have much fulfilment for me because I was a single mother, dating, fresh out of an abusive relationship *(YES, GIRL, I EVENTUALLY LEFT)*, and I wanted to see what I could truly do. My daddy started his business in the basement of his home, and it grew. I didn't need my dad's help; I was getting to the money *(Not really).* He was known to help the people in his neighborhood with their plumbing and heating issues, which was great, but that wasn't for me. I didn't fit in his business. However, life has a funny way of circling back to where we started, and for me, that circle began to close in the summer. I reluctantly stepped into his office to lend a hand. He immediately told me of his frustration and sadness that none of his children wanted to be a part of his business, even though I was the youngest and the only girl. He shared all of this with me. He laid this upon my shoulders. My introduction to the "family business" wasn't glamorous. My first day on the job my dad made me follow him through his office filled with people who don't look like me and led me *directly* to a dank cellar to digitize old contracts; I found myself battling dust, cobwebs, and a sinking feeling that this was a mistake. The pay was less than half of what I made braiding hair, and the isolation from the rest of the team only added to my frustration. I was pissed off, but I dare not say anything to my father about this because he was my dad and he is a former marine. Here we go again, talking about the *"1TS".* Because I had been taught about rank and order and because I was his "child", I could not address the way that I truly felt. My job was to scan old contracts and contract documents into the computer and then shred them. I did this for weeks on end while my allergies and sinuses suffered horribly. Yet, amidst this solitude and monotonous task, I stumbled upon my first real encounter with contracts, painstakingly scanning each document and inadvertently absorbing the language and terms that would later become my foundation in understanding business operations.

I was just about to quit because he was only paying me $8.50/hr when my computer and printer/scanner stopped working altogether. Transitioning from the cellar to working alongside the office manager, I was not greeted with hellos but rather with rolled eyes, sly comments and whispers. She and the others had made up their mind that I was a spoiled little daddy's girl with no experience and had no business in the midst of his business. Her dismissive attitude and lack of empathy for clients in need *highlighted a gap in the business* that I instinctively knew how to fill. This was a revelation for me. My makeshift customer service system, allowing customers to pay with post-dated checks, wasn't just a workaround; it was my first real impact on the business, blending morality with practicality. By month end, I had the service guys running with crazy calls because I had come up with a system. This experience, buried within the musty confines of a basement office, was a crash course in entrepreneurship. It taught me invaluable lessons about business, from **the importance of customer service** to the **intricacies of contract management**. More importantly, it was a lesson in resilience, *finding one's place in the most unexpected environments*, and *leveraging every challenge as a stepping stone toward personal and professional growth*.

As a young woman navigating the complexities of early adulthood, single motherhood, and the lingering shadows of an abusive past, these lessons in the basement laid the groundwork for the businesswoman I would become. It underscored the *necessity of resilience, the power of innovation* in the face of adversity, and the *importance of viewing every challenge as an opportunity to learn and evolve*.

For a minority, woman-owned business, my story is a testament to the fact that our beginnings, no matter how humble, are rich with lessons that can propel us forward. It's about recognizing that the barriers we face—whether they stem from societal biases, personal struggles, or the underestimated corners of a family business—can be transformed into the very strengths that define our success.

This chapter isn't just a recount of my first real job; it's an invitation to see beyond the immediate challenges and to find value in every experience. This was the beginning of my career. It's a reminder that the path to success is often paved with the bricks of our humble beginnings, each one laid down with lessons of perseverance, empathy, and unwavering determination.

Challenges and Solutions: Turning Hurdles into Stepping Stones

Life threw me into deep waters early on, and I had to learn how to swim. From job hopping to escaping an abusive relationship while juggling single motherhood, the challenges seemed endless. Yet, each obstacle taught me something crucial about life and business. Here's how I turned these challenges into lessons that fueled my journey as an entrepreneur.

Challenge 1: Finding Fulfillment Beyond Quick Money
Solution: Pursue passion with purpose. While quick gigs like hair braiding brought in fast cash, they lacked fulfillment. The real game-changer came when I embraced a role that aligned with my values, making a difference in my dad's business. The takeaway? Seek work that feeds your soul as well as your wallet.

Challenge 2: Stepping into Unfamiliar Territory
Solution: Embrace the learning curve. Initially resistant to working in my dad's plumbing business, I found myself in a dank basement, digitizing old contracts. This aggravating, seemingly unimportant task, unexpectedly laid the groundwork for my understanding of business operations. When you're out of your comfort zone, look for lessons in every task, no matter how small.

Challenge 3: Facing Workplace Isolation and Bias
Solution: Prove your worth through action. In an environment where I was judged for my youth and inexperience, I didn't let skepticism define me. By implementing a simple yet effective customer service solution, I demonstrated my value and changed my

perceptions. Don't wait for acceptance; earn it through innovation and results.

Challenge 4: Dealing with Personal Trauma While Building a Career
Solution: Draw strength from adversity. My personal experiences, including surviving domestic violence, taught me resilience that became invaluable in business. Use the strength you've gained from overcoming personal challenges to push through tough times in your professional life.

Turning Struggles Into Success: My Journey to Becoming a Boss

Starting from the bottom isn't just a catchy phrase from a song; it was my reality. Working in my dad's basement, feeling out of place, and coming up with creative fixes was like my own personal training ground for running a business. It wasn't just about getting through tough times; it was about learning how to stand strong, keep customers happy, and look at things differently. These tough times showed me that being a boss means more than just giving orders. It's about getting your hands dirty, understanding the nitty-gritty of your business, and showing love for every part of the work.

For me, a young Black woman trying to make it, these weren't just lessons; they hit deep. They taught me that making my own way, especially in a world that sometimes tries to put us in a corner, is not just necessary—it's vital. For us—minority folks, women, and veterans trying to build something of our own—we face extra challenges. But guess what? These challenges are actually our secret sauce. They teach us to be creative, to keep pushing, and to really feel what our customers need. That's what sets us apart when we step into the business world.

So, here's the real talk: My journey, with all its ups and downs, is proof that you can turn even the toughest situations into stepping stones for success. Every challenge, every setback, and every *'I got you'* moment is a chance to build something amazing. Success doesn't just pop up out of nowhere. It's built piece by piece, with hard work, a heart that understands others, and the kind of grit that keeps you moving forward, no matter what.

Remember, greatness starts in the most unexpected places, and building a dream is all about laying one brick at a time. So, let's keep laying those bricks with all the strength, love, and smarts we've got. That's how we build not just businesses but legacies.

Welcome to the Grind: The Blueprint to Building Your Empire

Hey babes! You've made it through the storm of the book, and now it's time to lay down the *bricks for your empire*. This next part of our journey together is where the real work begins. We're diving deep into the essentials of making your dream business a reality. From understanding the nitty-gritty of contracts to stretching every dollar in your budget, we're covering all bases. So, grab your notebook, 'cause trust me, you're gonna want to jot down these gems.

First up, we're gonna talk about Starting Your Real Business. This isn't just about having a great idea; it's about making it official, making it yours. We'll explore how to move from daydreams to real deals, step by step.

1. First, we will dive into the world of **Business Contracts.** Sounds fancy and a bit intimidating, right? But no stress, I'm gonna break it down so you know exactly what you're signing up for and *how to protect your hustle.*
2. **Effective Budget Management** is up next. Ever heard the saying, "It's not about how much you make but how much you keep"? We'll tackle *how to keep your cash flow healthy* so your business doesn't just grow; it thrives.
3. **Building a Support Network** is crucial. Nobody makes it alone, and you won't have to. I'll show you *how to find your tribe*, the folks who'll cheer you on, offer advice, and pick you up when you stumble.
4. **Marketing on a Budget?** Absolutely possible. I'll share creative, cost-effective ways to get the word out about your business without breaking the bank. Get ready to make some noise on the cheap.
5. We'll also talk about **Dealing with Failures and Setbacks**. Spoiler alert: *they're part of the journey*. But it's all about how you bounce back. I'll share personal stories of setbacks that seemed like the end but were really just the beginning.
6. **Celebrating Small Wins** is essential for keeping your spirits up. I'll remind you why every victory, no matter how tiny, is *a step towards your ultimate goal*.
7. And finally, **Work-Life Balance**. Yes, the *hustle is real, but so is burnout*. We'll explore ways to manage

your time so your business grows without you wearing out.

This part of the book is your ***Daily Grind Guide.*** It's packed with practical advice, real-life lessons, and tons of encouragement. So, **pay close attention**, **take notes**, and get ready to **put in the work**. Your empire isn't going to build itself, but with a little sweat, a lot of smarts, and a huge heart, you'll get there. ***Let's do this!***

Chapter 7:

Laying the Groundwork for Your Empire"

So, you've got that fire in your heart to start something of your own. You're ready to take that leap and make your business more than just a side hustle or a dream. It's time to make it real and legit and set it up for success. This chapter is all about turning that vision into a solid foundation, especially for us in the Black community and our brothers and sisters who are women and veterans. Let's get into how you can start your *REAL* business the right way.

Making Your Business Legit

First things first, you gotta make your business official. Think of it like this: just like you wouldn't drive a car without getting it registered, you shouldn't run a business without making it legit. The easiest and quickest way to do this? Setting up an LLC or Limited Liability Company. It's like putting a protective bubble around your personal assets (like your car or house) so that if your business faces any issues, you're not personally on the hook. You can do this by going to your Business' Department of State or Secretary of State.

Choosing the Right Structure

An LLC is cool because it's flexible and doesn't need a ton of paperwork to get started. But before you dive in, you gotta understand what kind of business you're running. Are you *selling products like T-shirts or beauty supplies?* Or are you *offering services like graphic design* or *hair styling*? Knowing this will help you figure out the best structure for your company and what licenses and permits you need to keep things smooth.

Licenses, Permits, and Taxes, Oh My!

Depending on what you're selling or what service you're providing, you might need specific licenses and permits. It's like having the right key to open the door to your business. And don't forget about setting up sales tax and getting a Tax Identification Number (EIN) from the IRS. This isn't just about paying taxes; it's your business's ID, like how your Social Security number is your personal ID.

Making It Official for Minorities, Women, and Veterans

For us minorities, women, and veterans, it's super important to set up our businesses properly. Not only does it add credibility, but it also opens up opportunities for loans, grants, and contracts that are specifically designed to support our growth. It's like having VIP access to resources that can help elevate our businesses.

Raising the Money

Now, let's talk money. If your pockets are light, don't stress. There are ways to raise the funds to kickstart your business. *Crowdfunding, small business grants,* and *loans* specifically for minorities, women, and veterans can be a good start. It's all about being resourceful and tapping into the networks and opportunities available to us.

The Daily Grind

Remember, *setting up your business is just the beginning*. There's daily work involved in making sure everything runs like a well-oiled machine. From **managing your finances** to **keeping up with paperwork**, the **hustle never stops**. But trust me, it's all worth it when you see your business thriving and making an impact.

Starting your real business as a Black entrepreneur, or as a woman and/or veteran, is about more than just making money. It's about building something that lasts, creates value, and represents our communities. By setting up your business properly, you're laying down the foundation for something great. It's a journey filled with challenges but also with victories. So, take these steps seriously, put in the work, and watch as your business grows from a dream into a legacy. Let's build these empires, y'all!

I know we only scratched the surface on these items, and for some of those items, that is more than enough for you to get going in your business, but for some of us who need a little more detail, this next section is for you. This will be a 2 part section because I want to be sure you complete one step before the next. I almost spilled the tea on the next part... You know what, never mind. Let's get to it.

"Choosing Your Hustle's Home: Understanding Business Structures"

ILet's elevate on the real deal about starting your business: *picking the right structure*. It's like choosing the best outfit for a big event; you *MUST* know your options and what works best for you. I'll break it down and keep it simple, so that you can figure out which setup will have your business looking sharp and protected.

Sole Proprietorship
Think of a sole proprietorship as your solo act. It's just you running the show.

Pros: It's super easy to start, and you're in complete control. Plus, you keep all the profits.

Cons: The downside? Your personal assets (like your car or house) are on the line if your business gets into debt or legal issues.

Partnership
A partnership is like forming a team. You and at least one other person share ownership of the business.

Pros: You've got someone to share the workload and brainstorm with. Plus, each partner brings their skills and resources to the table.

Cons: But remember, you also share the risks. And sometimes, working closely with someone else can lead to disagreements.

Corporation (C-Corp)
A corporation is the big leagues, setting your business up as its own legal entity.

Pros: The biggest win here is that your personal stuff is safe from business debts or lawsuits. Plus, you can sell stock to raise money.

Cons: The trade-off? It's more complex to set up, and you're looking at more rules, regulations, and taxes.

Limited Liability Company (LLC)
An LLC mixes some of the best parts of sole proprietorships, partnerships, and corporations.

Pros: Your personal assets are protected, and it's flexible. You can choose how you want to be taxed (like a sole proprietor, partnership, or corporation).

Cons: Setting it up can be more complicated and expensive than a sole proprietorship or partnership.

DBA (Doing Business As)
DBA is like your business's nickname. It doesn't change how your business is structured but lets you operate under a different name.

Pro Tip: While a DBA lets you use a catchy name, it doesn't give you legal protection. Your personal assets are still on the hook if you're a sole proprietor or in a general partnership.

Why Delaware, though?

Now, here's a pro tip you might hear floating around: setting up your business in Delaware. Why? Delaware is like the VIP section for businesses.

Benefits: The state has some of the most business-friendly laws out there.

1. It offers strong protection for your personal assets.
2. Has flexible business laws
3. Even if you don't live there, you can still set up shop.
4. Plus, the court system in Delaware is super experienced with business issues, which can be a big plus if you ever need legal help.

Choosing the right business structure is like picking the right tool for the job. It's all about what fits your situation best, keeping your assets safe, and planning for the future of your hustle. Remember, each structure has its own set of pros and cons, so think about what you need, what you want to protect, and how big you dream of growing. And don't sleep on the Delaware tip; sometimes, the best home for your business might not be your home state. *Keep these insights in your back pocket as you build your empire, step by step.*

<u>Naming Your Dream: The Heartbeat of Your Brand"</u>
Oooh this is one of my favorite parts. Let's talk about something super important but often rushed—picking your business name. I remember when I was thinking of opening my first salon, I just knew what the name of the salon would be; it was easy. I was going to name it after my daughter, and that was it. Her name is different and sounded a little French " Marja'e kind of like Targe't) Oh naw. Oh, ok, anyway. Fast forward to 18 years later, and I have three children, girls by the way. Imagine how they would've felt with that name. Not that it was a bad idea or that it wouldn't have worked, but let's just elevate and elaborate on this a bit.

Think of your business name as the first hello to your future customers. It's more than just a label; it's the first chapter of your business story, the vibe you're sending out to the world. So, it's crucial to give it the thought and respect it deserves. Here are some dos and don'ts to consider when naming your baby—*ahem*, I mean your business.

Dos of Business Naming:

1. *Keep It Memorable but Simple*: You want a name that sticks in people's minds but isn't a tongue-twister. If folks can remember and say your business name easily, you're off to a good start.
2. *Reflect Your Brand:* Your name should give people a clue about what you do. It's like a sneak peek into the services or products you offer. Make it relevant to your hustle.
3. *Do Your Research*: Make sure your name isn't already taken, especially by a business in your field. A quick internet search and a look through the trademark database can save you a lot of headaches later.
4. *Future-Proof It:* Choose a name that can grow with your business. You might start with cupcakes but dream of expanding to full-on catering. Pick a name that won't box you in.
5. *Get Feedback:* Run your favorite names by people you trust. Sometimes, an outside perspective can spot things you missed or confirm you're on the right track.

So now that we have the Dos down packed, we must get into the Don'ts, and this is super important. I know a friend of a friend who has a very ghetto business name, but I respect it, and the name is memorable; I will literally NEVER forget the name. But at some point, you have to know where to draw the line, and then I have a friend of a friend with a very sexualized business name, and it's a construction company, and it's like, "Girl, relax 'we get it. But are you coming to do the construction or coming to entice somebody's husband? *I'm joking, but seriously.* Your name is very important.

Don'ts of Business Naming:

- *Avoid Hard-to-Spell Names* If people need to Google your business name every time because they can't remember how to spell it, that's a problem.
- *Don't Be Too Narrow*: Avoid names that limit your business to a specific product or city unless you're sure you won't expand beyond that.
- *Steer Clear of Trends*: What's cool today might be outdated tomorrow. Aim for a name that's timeless.
- *Don't Forget the Domain:* In today's digital world, having an online presence is key. Check if the domain name for your business is available. You want a website name that matches your business name.
- *Don't Rush It:* Take your time. Your business name is a big deal and worth mulling over until you find the perfect fit.

Why Your Business Name and Branding Matter:

Your business name is the cornerstone of your brand. It's how customers will find you, remember you, and start to build a relationship with you. Good branding, with a strong, fitting name, sets the tone for everything else—from your logo to your website to the way you package your products or services. It's about creating a vibe, an identity that people can connect with.

So, take a breath and give this process the attention it deserves. Your business name is the first step in sharing your vision with the world. Make it count. This isn't just about making a mark; it's about making the right mark. Remember, your business name is out there doing work for you even when you're not. It's calling out to potential customers, making a first impression, and starting a story that you'll be telling for years to come. Let's make it a story worth telling.

I hope this chapter has helped you make a decision on what business structure is right for you and have you thinking about your business name, branding, etc. It's important to know this information before jumping in head first. I'm so excited that you are doing the work of knowing. Here's a little secret: most of us start businesses without ever having a piece of paperwork. If you're like me, you started as a kid just fooling around with hair, or maybe you jumped into the kitchen because your mom had a new mixer; if you're like my girl Gabby. She is an amazing cake baker. I remember asking her how she got into cake making, and I'm not sharing her business, well maybe just a little, but she told me it was because her mother won on a home makeover show, and the kitchen had baking appliances in it, and she just began to bake. Listen, when I tell you she is incredible, I truly mean that. Before I opened up my salon, I worked out of my home to see if I was actually disciplined enough to work in a salon setting. I built up my clientele and even went back to cosmetology school for a 3rd time to brush up on my skills and ensure that I was up to date on the latest styling techniques, tools, equipment, and products. Anywhoo, y'all know that I can go on all day with my millions of experiences, but this next chapter is very near and dear to my heart, so if you are a

Small, Disadvantaged, minority, woman or veteran-owned company, please strap on your seat belts so that we can dive into a life-changing chapter.

"Unlocking Doors: The Power of Certifying Your Business"

Hey, y'all, hey!!! Let's elevate on something that could be a game-changer for your hustle: getting your business certified as minority, woman, or veteran-owned. Why is this a big deal? Well, it's like getting a key to a whole new set of opportunities that can help take your business to the next level. Let's break it down and see why it's crucial for us to get this right. This is so important to your business, and I'm so excited to drop these jewels that I'm about to burst.

The VIP Pass: Certification Benefits

When you certify your business as minority, woman, or veteran-owned (think MWBE for Minority and Women-Owned Business Enterprises and VOSB for Veteran-Owned Small Business), it's like wearing a badge of honor. But it's more than just respect; it's about what that badge can get you:

Credibility: It shows the world, especially big companies and the government, that your business is legit and ready to play in the big leagues.

Access to Special Loans, Grants, and Contracts: There are lots of money and contracts set aside just for businesses like ours. We're talking about loans with better rates, grants to help us grow, and contracts that can keep our businesses busy and profitable.

Networking Opportunities: These certifications open doors to networking events where you can meet other business owners like you, share experiences, and even find mentors.

The MWBE and VOSB Programs

The government and some big companies are on a mission to spend more money with businesses run by minorities, women, and veterans. Why? Because for too long, we've been left out of the loop. The MWBE and VOSB programs are about leveling the playing field and making sure we get a fair shot at contracts and opportunities.

Did you know the government spends billions (yes, billions with a 'B') every year with small businesses? That's a lot of dough; it could be going to businesses like yours. But to get in on this, you need to be certified.

Not Just a Handout: Building Credibility and Relationships

Here's the real talk: these programs aren't just about giving us a slice of the pie. They're about showing what we can do, proving our worth, and building long-lasting relationships. The goal isn't to rely on these programs forever but to use them as a stepping stone to get our businesses to a place where we're competing and winning based on our skills, products, and services.

A Call to Action: Get Certified, Get Connected, Get Going

So, what's the next move? If you're running a business and you're a minority, woman, or veteran, it's time to get certified.

Look into the MWBE and VOSB programs, see what you need to do to get that certification, and start opening doors to new opportunities. Be sure to connect with **www.themwbecoach.com**, where you will be able to find answers to commonly asked certification questions. Links to certification in your state and a certification support group: ALSO, I launched the NEW YORK STATE MWBE Certification coaching course. Yes, Yes. YASSSS!!! Feel free to

Step 1: Research the certification process for your state or the federal government.

Step 2: Gather your documents and apply. It might take a bit of paperwork, but it's worth it.

Step 3: Once you're certified, start applying for those contracts and use the networks and resources available to you. You can follow me on **TikTok and Instagram @TheMWBECoach**. I post loads of videos with free assistance, and we run a monthly meeting that helps you get your business order...

Your Business, Your Future

Certifying your business is about taking control of your future. It's a powerful step towards showing the world the value of what you've built. So, let's get your businesses certified, let's win those contracts, and let's show everyone what we're made of. This is our time to shine, grow, and create legacies that will last for generations. Let's do this!

Chapter 8:

First Impressions: Landing Your First Customer"

This may be one of the most exciting parts of starting your business—getting that very first customer. This moment is more than just a sale; it's the start of your journey to making your dream a reality. It's about putting those boots on the ground and showing the world what you've got.

The Boots on the Ground Approach
First things first, you've got to get out there. Remember how we talked about picking the perfect name for your business? That name is your first hello to the world. Now, it's time to introduce yourself properly. Whether it's hitting the pavement, attending community events, or showcasing your business at local markets, your presence and your hustle make all the difference. This approach isn't just about being seen; it's about making meaningful connections.

Appeal to Your Audience
Knowing who you're selling to is key. Once you've named your business in a way that resonates, it's time to dial into what your audience really wants and needs. Talk to them, listen to their feedback, and tailor your pitch to highlight how your product or service solves their problems. Remember, you're not just selling something; you're offering a solution, a better way.

Become the Salesperson You Never Knew You Could Be

Now, for many of us, especially minorities and women, selling doesn't come naturally. Our backgrounds and experiences might have us fearing rejection and worrying about hearing "no." But here's the thing—every "no" is a step closer to a "yes." Sales is about perseverance, about believing in your product or service so much that this belief becomes contagious. You've got to wear your passion on your sleeve and let it speak for you. Don't go into the world feeling that you need sale yourself, instead go in knowing that you have a product or a service that is solving a problem. That is the key to sales. Be sure that you are connecting with your client/ customer.

Breaking Through the Fear

It's normal to feel scared or even depressed when things don't take off right away. But remember, you're made of tougher stuff. The very fact that you've started this journey shows you've got what it takes. Push through the doubt, keep reaching out, and let your dedication shine. People are drawn to authenticity and passion—it's your best selling point. If you are natural introverted and you just can't bring yourself to do it, imagine that every person you speak to is the mirror. If it's still too overwhelming, consider asking one of your friends or family to be a sales representative for your product or service.

The Power of Word of Mouth and Referrals

Never underestimate the power of a happy customer. Word of mouth is golden in this game. When someone loves what you do, they'll talk, and their words carry weight.

Encourage referrals by providing exceptional service and maybe even incentives for customers who bring in new business. A recommendation from a satisfied customer is priceless—it's personal, trusted, and, best of all, free.

Landing your first customer is a milestone, but it's also just the beginning. Every interaction, every pitch, and every sale is a chance to learn and grow. Keep your head up, stay true to your mission, and remember why you started this journey. Your first customer won't be your last if you keep putting in the work, making those connections, and believing in what you have to offer.

So, lace up those boots, get out there, and make that first impression count. Your dream awaits you to make it real, one customer at a time. Let's get it!

Chapter 9:

Contract Smarts: Navigating Agreements Without Getting Burned

Are you still with me, or are you feeling a bit overwhelmed? If you are overwhelmed, relax a bit and unwind. Music is my therapy, and I promise you that you are more than halfway done. Take some time to go back and check out The Official Marja'e on YouTube. Refill that cup if you need to. Coffee keeps you up, but try some mushroom coffee for the focus or whatever you can handle. Are you Good? Okay, cool. Let's talk contracts. I know, just hearing the word might make your eyes glaze over, but stick with me. Understanding business contracts is like knowing the rules of the game—you might not love it, but you gotta know it to play and win. Let me share a bit of my journey and some real talk on the dos and don'ts of dealing with contracts so you don't have to learn the hard way like I did.

My First Contract Flop

I remember signing my first business contract. I was buzzing with excitement, so much so that I didn't read the whole thing. Big mistake. That oversight ended up costing me a customer and taught me a lesson I'll never forget. I made a deal for a flooring job, but it didn't get specific enough in the contract, and when the customer wanted changes, we just shook on it: no written updates, no change orders—nothing. And when the bamboo floors we installed got scuffed (which bamboo does easily), guess who she blamed? Yep, me. She even pulled out the "30-

day warranty" card from the contract I hadn't scrutinized closely. It was a mess, and it hit my wallet hard.

The Dos of Contracts

Read Every Word: Treat your contract like a map to buried treasure. Every single word matters because, in the end, they protect your treasure—your business.

Get Specific: Be as detailed as possible. What are you delivering? When? How? Specify materials, deadlines, payment schedules—everything. The devil's in the details, and those details save you from headaches later.

Change Orders Are Your Friend: Changes happen, but always document them with a change order. This piece of paper can be your best friend, proving what was agreed upon if memories suddenly get fuzzy.

The Don'ts of Contracts

Don't Skip the Fine Print: It might be boring, but the fine print is where some of the most critical pieces of your agreement live. Skipping it is like skipping training and heading straight to the championship game.

Don't Assume Good Intentions Replace Paperwork: Handshake deals might feel honorable, but they won't stand up in court. Protect yourself and your business with documented agreements.

Don't Forget to Plan for the Worst: Hope for the best, but plan for the worst. Include clauses for late payments, cancellations, and warranties. It's not pessimistic; it's smart.

The Importance of Dotting I's and Crossing T's

Whether you're dealing with residential, commercial, or government contracts, the importance of being thorough can't be overstressed. Every detail, no matter how small it seems, should be in writing. This isn't just about covering your back; it's about respecting your work and ensuring you're paid and treated fairly.

Your Takeaway

Contracts might seem daunting, but they're just part of the business game. They're here to protect you, your customers, and the integrity of your work. Take the time to understand them, get comfortable with the lingo, and don't be afraid to ask questions or get a professional to review them before you sign.

This chapter isn't just a lesson; it's a call to action. Treat your contracts with the seriousness they deserve, and you'll build a foundation of trust and professionalism that can take your business to the next level. Remember, a well-crafted contract is a sign of a pro who means business, and that's exactly what you are. Let's get to work and make sure we're not just doing business but doing it right.

Chapter 10:

Stretching Dollars: Mastering Your Business Budget

If you are in business, thinking about starting a business, heck, if you're living life, this is something we all gotta deal with but might not always love talking about—money specifically, how to manage your business budget when it feels like you're trying to stretch a dollar into a twenty. For minority and women-owned businesses, getting our money right isn't just good practice; it's essential for keeping our dreams alive and thriving. Let's break down how to make the most of what we've got and grow from there.

Problem Statement:

For many of us starting or running our businesses, the financial runway might seem short. We're often working with less - less capital, less access to traditional funding sources, and less cushion for errors. This can make or break us, especially in the early stages. So, how do we flip the script and turn our financial limitations into strengths?

Here are some crucial solutions and steps:

Understand Your Cash Flow:

Do: Keep track of every dollar coming in and going out. This helps you see the bigger picture and make smarter decisions.

Tool Tip: Use free or low-cost budgeting apps or software to keep tabs on your finances.

Trim the Fat:

Do: Look for areas where you can cut costs without cutting corners. Maybe it's negotiating with suppliers or cutting unnecessary subscriptions.

Tool Tip: Always ask for discounts or bulk purchase deals. You'd be surprised how often you can get a price cut just by asking.

Smart Funding Options:

Credit Unions and Community Banks: Often more willing to work with small businesses, they may offer better rates and more personalized service than big banks.

Crowdfunding: Platforms like Kickstarter or GoFundMe can be a way to raise funds for a project without taking on debt.

Microloans: Organizations like Kiva offer microloans that can be easier to qualify for than traditional bank loans.

Building Bank Relationships:

Do: Start building relationships with local banks or credit unions. Even if you don't need a loan right now, establishing a history can help down the line.

Tool Tip: Schedule a meeting with a bank's small business advisor to discuss your business and financial goals.

Credit Management:

Do: Work on improving your personal and business credit scores. Pay bills on time, keep debt levels manageable, and monitor your credit report for errors.

Tool Tip: Consider a secured credit card for your business to build credit if you're starting from scratch.

Emergency Fund:

Do: Aim to save enough to cover at least 3-6 months of operating expenses. This gives you a buffer for unexpected challenges.

Tool Tip: Set aside a small percentage of every sale into your emergency fund. Treat it like another business expense.

Lean Operations:

Do: Run your business as lean as possible. Focus on what brings in revenue and cut or outsource the rest.
Tool Tip: Use freelancers or temporary help for tasks outside your core business to save on payroll costs.
The Importance of Being Financially Savvy:

In a world where access to resources isn't always equal, being smart with our money isn't just a skill—it's our **superpower**. It's about making every dollar work harder for us so we can focus on growing our businesses and making an impact.

Let me share a story that hits right at the heart of why knowing how to manage your budget is more than just number crunching—it's about making your dreams happen, even when the odds seem stacked against you.

There I was, blessed with a golden opportunity: a large contract that was a game-changer for my business. It was the kind of break I'd been praying for. But with great opportunities come big challenges. To pull this off, I needed to bring on five new employees, secure new insurance, and cover lodging in another city. Sounds straightforward, right? Well, there was a catch—I had no formal business credit line, and my personal credit was just okay. It's not exactly the ideal situation when you need a financial boost.

Now, here's where things got interesting. I had to think fast and smart. So, I went to OneMain Financial and secured a high-interest loan. Yes, the interest was steep, but the contract payment terms were in my favor—I'd be paid in 30 days, which meant I could repay the loan before those hefty interest fees kicked in. And that's exactly what happened. I took the leap, managed the project carefully, and when that paycheck came in, I cleared the loan without losing extra money on interest.

But the story doesn't end there. The contract got extended *(talk about blessings flowing!),* and I found myself needing financial help again. This time, armed with the experience and a bit more savvy, I turned to my credit union, where I'd been building a relationship. Thanks to that connection, I was able to secure a personal loan with much better terms. This wasn't just about the money; it was a testament to the power of building solid relationships with financial institutions.

Here's the takeaway from my journey:

Build Relationships with Financial Institutions: Whether it's a credit union or a local bank, start building that relationship early. When you're in a pinch, these relationships can be your lifeline.

Understand the Terms of Your Loans: High-interest loans can be a quick fix, but they come with risks. Always have a repayment plan in place to avoid getting trapped by interest fees.

Use Opportunities to Build Your Credit: Every time you successfully repay a loan, it's a win for your credit score. Better credit opens up better opportunities for funding in the future.

Be Prepared for the Unexpected: Opportunities don't always come with advance notice. Being financially savvy means you can jump on them without hesitation.

Don't Let 'No' Stop You: If one door closes, knock on another. There are financial products and institutions out there willing to work with you. Keep looking until you find the right fit.

This chapter isn't just about managing a budget; it's about strategically leveraging your resources to not only keep your business running but to propel it forward. My experience taught me that with a little creativity, a lot of hustle, and the right financial partners, you can turn even the most daunting challenges into stepping stones for your business's success. Let's keep pushing, growing, and remembering that our dreams are worth every effort.

Remember, it's not about having a lot of money but about making the most of what you have. With the right strategies, a clear understanding of your finances, and a bit of creativity, you can build a financial foundation that will support your business now and in the future. Let's make our financial health a priority and watch as our businesses flourish because of it.

Chapter 11:

We're Stronger Together: Building a Support Network

In the journey of entrepreneurship, especially for us in the African American community, the road can sometimes feel lonely. We're often pioneering our paths, breaking barriers, and facing challenges head-on. But here's the thing—while our individuality is our strength, isolation can be our kryptonite. The truth is that many Black-owned businesses face a common hurdle: the struggle to scale and secure larger contracts. This all goes back to a capacity building aspect. This isn't just about competition but collaboration—or the lack thereof. The biggest projects often go to those who can show they have the capacity and the qualifications to deliver, and too many times, our businesses miss out because we're seen as 'too small' or 'not ready.' I want to elevate on some solutions to this very common issue, especially in government contracting.

1. Solutions for Building Strength in Numbers

Collaborate to Amplify Capacity: The largest companies out there didn't get to where they are by going at it alone. They joined forces, pooled resources, and tackled projects that would've been out of reach solo. Imagine the impact if more Black-owned businesses did the same. I remember waking up one morning and seeing that 3 very large businesses, in the same arena, decided to join forces. I began sending text messages to my family, but no one answered the call and this is all too common in our communities. Collaboration can amplify our capacity and make us contenders for big contracts.

Invest in Networking: Building meaningful relationships with like-minded business owners isn't just good for morale; it's strategic. Networking can open doors to partnerships, mentorship, and opportunities that we might not find on our own. You never know who you are in the room with. One connection is worth the money and time it takes to network.

2. The Power of a Support Network

Networking isn't just about swapping business cards; it's about weaving a fabric of support that lifts all involved. It's about creating a community where knowledge, resources, and opportunities can flow freely. The statistics are clear: businesses that lean on each other and share insights and resources stand a better chance of thriving. *For African American businesses, this is crucial*. The power of collaboration is *undeniable* yet *underutilized*. By joining forces, we can take on larger projects, navigate the complexities of securing contracts, and push each other towards greater achievements.

My Story: Navigating Government Contracts
Let me share a bit of my journey. Trying to secure government contracts as a minority, woman, and veteran-owned business has been an eye-opener. The government wants to work with us, but the boxes we need to tick— *'qualified,' 'capable,' 'ready'*—are often just out of reach for a small business going it alone. I learned the hard way that if we pool our resources, bring our unique strengths to the

table, and present a united front, not only does it increase our chances of winning these contracts, but it also elevates all our businesses. It's a win-win. Here I was presented with an opportunity to go after a large government contract and I said **** it, I'm going to do this alone. I had a mentor session booked but, honestly, I did not need another woman who was only going to judge me and pretend that she knows my struggle, giving me business advice. I went ahead and logged into the online meeting and she, literally, did my black owned business dishes. Not only was she inspiring but she was sweet, genuine and just all around amazing. This lady is Stacie Alexiou with Watts and Flux. She gave me great advice, she coached me and offered to partner with me on the same project that I was afraid to do on my own, but I was taking the risk. Why did I put that bit into my book? Because I had given up on there being any good in us. I was burnt out from other experiences and out her into a box. Her knowledge and kindness, literally, distinguished my fire. I said all of this a segway into the next point.

Making the Most of Networking Opportunities
Networking doesn't have to break the bank. It's about choosing the right events and making each opportunity count.

Budget Wisely: Set aside a portion of your budget for networking. Think of it as an investment in your business's future.

Choose Strategically: Not all networking events are created equal. Look for events that align with your business goals and have a track record of fostering genuine connections.

Prepare to Engage: Before attending an event, know what you want to get out of it. Have your elevator pitch ready, and be open to learning and sharing.

A Call to Unity

Building a support network is more than a strategy; it's a necessity. It's about recognizing that our collective power is far greater than what we can achieve alone. This is what my dear coach, Stacie taught me. By fostering collaboration, investing in our community, and embracing the power of networking, we set the stage for a future where minority, women and veteran-owned businesses don't just survive; they thrive. Let's commit to building bridges, sharing successes, and, most importantly, lifting each other up. Together, we're unstoppable.

Chapter 12:

Joining Forces: Crafting Meaningful Partnerships

Welcome to the chapter on "Crafting Meaningful Partnerships," where we're diving into the art of building relationships that matter in business. In this section, we'll explore how to forge connections that go beyond transactions, creating partnerships that are rooted in shared values, mutual respect, and a common vision for success. Get ready to learn how to navigate the world of collaboration with confidence and authenticity, as we uncover the secrets to building partnerships that truly make a difference. This is something super important but often overlooked—how we, as minority and women-owned businesses, can reach out to others for partnerships that don't just look good on paper but actually work wonders in reality. Building bridges and forming alliances can catapult our businesses to new heights. But how do we do it right? Let's break it down.

Initiating the Partnership Dance

1.*Identify Potential Partners:* Start by looking for businesses that complement yours. Think about what you're good at and where you could use support. The goal here is synergy, where 1+1 equals way more than 2.

2.*Do Your Homework:* Before you approach anyone, do a deep dive into their business. Understand their goals, their customer base, and their values. This shows you're serious and not just shooting in the dark.

3.**Make the First Move:** Reach out with a clear, concise, and compelling message. Share why you think a partnership could be beneficial and suggest a casual meeting to discuss the idea further. This could be a coffee chat or a virtual meet-up — keep it low-pressure

Forming Meaningful Partnerships

1.**Shared Values and Vision:** The foundation of any strong partnership is alignment in values and vision. You're looking for a partner who not only complements your business but also shares your broader goals and ethics.

2.**Clear Communication:** From the get-go, establish open lines of communication. This means being honest about expectations, fears, and hopes. It's all about building trust.

3.**Define Roles and Responsibilities:** Be crystal clear about who is doing what. This clarity prevents overlap, confusion, and frustration down the line.

Knowing You've Found the Right Partner

1.**Mutual Respect:** You know you've found the right partner when there's mutual respect. You value each other's expertise, listen to each other's opinions, and support each other's growth.

2.**Excitement for the Future:** When discussions about potential projects get you both excited, that's a good sign. It means you're on the same wavelength about what you can achieve together.

3.**Ease of Communication:** Conversations flow easily, decisions are reached without much conflict, and you find yourselves on the same page more often than not.

Steps to Successful Collaboration

1.**Set Common Goals:** Begin by setting goals that are beneficial to both parties. This ensures you're working towards a shared outcome.

2.**Draft a Partnership Agreement:** It might seem formal, but having a written agreement lays out the expectations, roles, and financials clearly, preventing issues down the line.

3.**Plan for Conflict Resolution:** Agree on how you'll handle disagreements before they arise. Having a strategy in place helps navigate conflicts constructively.

4.**Celebrate Wins Together:** Acknowledge and celebrate your successes. This reinforces the value of your partnership and keeps morale high.

5.**Evaluate and Adjust:** Regularly check the partnership's progress. Be open to adjusting your approach as your businesses evolve.

Stronger Together

Remember, the goal of forming partnerships isn't just to expand your business but to build a community where we all lift each other up. By approaching potential partners thoughtfully, forming alliances based on shared values, and navigating the partnership with clear communication and mutual respect, we set ourselves up for success. Let's not shy away from reaching out. In unity, there's strength, and together, we can achieve incredible things. Here's to building partnerships that propel us forward and make our entrepreneurial dreams a reality.

Chapter 13:

Ballin' on a Budget: Marketing Magic for Your Business

We are jamming through this book and I hope that you are staying with me. We are diving into another one of my favorite topics—making the most out of marketing without breaking the bank. We all know money doesn't grow on trees, and when you're hustling to grow your business, every dollar counts. I want to share how I've leveraged the power of social media and good ol' word of mouth to build my brands and how you can do the same, no matter what you're working with.

My Marketing Journey: Social Media & Word of Mouth

From the jump, I knew I had to get creative with how I spread the word about my businesses. Traditional advertising? *Expensive.* Billboards? *Out of the question.* So, I turned to social media and the power of community chatter. Yes, those social media algorithms are like shifting sands, but one thing remains constant—the need for consistency. Regular posts, engaging content, and staying true to my brand have been key. And when it comes to rebranding? *I've done it more times than I can count*, but each time, I make sure that my brand's essence shines through, from my website to my business cards.

Pro Tips for Marketing on a Shoestring Budget

<u>Consistency is Key:</u> Keep your posts regular. You don't need to post every hour but find a rhythm that works for you and stick to it. Consistency helps you stay on your audience's radar.

<u>Engagement Over Everything:</u> Talk to your followers, not at them. Respond to comments, ask questions, and create content that invites conversation. The more engaged your audience is, the more likely they are to spread the word.

<u>Leverage Free Tools:</u> There are tons of free tools out there designed to help you create stunning social media posts, track your engagement, and manage your content calendar. Use them to your advantage.

<u>Be Authentic:</u> People connect with realness. Share your story, the highs and the lows. Authenticity builds trust, and trust leads to loyal customers.

<u>Word of Mouth is Golden:</u> Never underestimate the power of a happy customer. Encourage them to share their experiences with their network. Sometimes, a personal recommendation is the most powerful marketing tool you have.

<u>Rebrand with Purpose:</u> If you're pivoting or expanding, make sure your rebranding efforts are clear, intentional, and communicated well across all your platforms. Consistency in your brand image and message helps maintain trust and recognition.

<u>Match Your Materials:</u> Ensure your online presence and physical marketing materials (like business cards) tell the

same story. A cohesive brand image is visually appealing and reinforces your identity.

Network, Network, Network: Get involved in community events, online forums, and social media groups relevant to your industry. Networking can lead to partnerships, collaborations, and exposure to new audiences.

The Bottom Line: Making It Work for You
The truth is that marketing doesn't have to be about who has the biggest budget. It's about *who has the clearest message*, the most consistent presence, and the ability to genuinely connect with their audience. I've built my companies with these principles, focusing on creating a brand that resonates and engages.

So, whether you're a one-person show or a growing team, remember: your story is powerful, your brand is unique, and your determination can make all the difference. Let's use what we've got to make some noise and let the world know we're here. It's time to market like a boss, even when the budget is tight. Let's get it!

Chapter 14:

Heart to Heart: Connecting Through Your Story

There is so much that goes into the power of sharing your story, the art of engaging with your audience, and the magic of referrals. Let's keep it real—our journeys, with all their ups and downs, are what make us unique. And in the world of business, especially for us in the African American community, being open and transparent can truly set us apart.

The Power of Sharing Your Story

Being transparent about your journey doesn't just add layers to your brand; it builds bridges to your audience. When you share where you've been, the challenges you've overcome, and the victories you've celebrated, you're not just selling a product or service; you're inviting your audience into your world. This connection? *It's priceless.*

Engaging With Your Audience on Social Media
Social media is like the modern-day marketplace—it's where conversations happen, relationships are built, and stories are shared. Here's how you can make the most of it:

Quizzes and Polls: People love sharing their opinions. Use quizzes or polls to spark conversations and learn more about what your audience cares about.

Ask Questions: It's simple but effective. Asking your followers questions encourages them to interact directly with your brand. Plus, it shows you value their input.

Share Behind-the-Scenes Content: Let your audience peek behind the curtain. Whether it's the making of a product or a day in your life, these glimpses create a deeper connection.

<u>Consistency in Your Branding</u>
When it comes to branding, consistency is key. Using the same colors, fonts, and style across all your platforms isn't just about looking polished—it's about being recognizable. Your audience should be able to see a post or an ad and immediately know it's you without even seeing your logo. This visual consistency makes your brand memorable and trusted.The Referral Game

Referrals have been a game-changer for my business, and they can be for yours too. Here's how:

BOGO and Discounted Promotions: Offering a 'Buy One, Get One 'or a discount for returning customers encourages folks to spread the word about your business. It's a win-win; they get a deal, and you get exposure.

Referral Rewards: Show appreciation to those who refer new clients your way. Whether it's a discount, a small gift, or a shoutout on social media, acknowledging their support fosters loyalty and encourages more referrals.

Partner Up: Collaborate with other businesses or influencers who share your audience. They can introduce your brand to their followers, expanding your reach.

Making Connections That Count

At the end of the day, business is about more than transactions; it's about relationships. By sharing your story with authenticity, engaging with your audience in meaningful ways, maintaining a consistent brand image, and leveraging the power of referrals, you're not just building a customer base—you're building a community. And in this community, every heart you touch, every conversation you start, and every relationship you build brings you one step closer to not just achieving your business goals but surpassing them. Let's keep it real; let's stay connected, and let's grow together.

Champions of Your Brand: Unlocking the Power of Brand Ambassadors

Let's elevate about something that can really amplify your business's voice on social media without needing to dig deep into your pockets—brand ambassadors. Whether you're just starting or looking to boost your existing business, understanding how to leverage brand ambassadors can be a game-changer. So, what's the deal with brand ambassadors, and how can they help your hustle? Let's dive in.

Who Are Brand Ambassadors?

Think of brand ambassadors as your *business's biggest fans and supporters*. They're the folks who love what you do so much that they're excited to talk about it on their social media platforms. This could be through Instagram stories, tweets, Facebook posts, or TikTok videos. *They're like your hype crew*, spreading the word about your products or services to their followers, which can seriously expand your reach.

What Types of Businesses Benefit?

Honestly? *Just about any business can benefit from having brand ambassadors.* Whether you're selling handcrafted jewelry, running a catering service, offering personal training, or anything in between, having real people share their genuine love for what you do can make others take notice. It's all about connecting with folks who resonate with your brand and can authentically share that vibe with others.

The Magic of Free Marketing Strategies

Now, onto more ways to market your business on a budget because we all know every dollar counts. Alongside leveraging brand ambassadors, here are some free strategies to get your name out there:

Social Media Presence: Keep your social media game strong. Regular, engaging posts that reflect your brand's personality can attract followers organically.

Collaborations: Team up with other businesses or influencers for shoutouts or collaborations. It's a win-win as both parties get exposed to each other's audiences.

Content Creation: Blog posts, how-to videos, and other valuable content can draw people to your brand. Plus, it positions you as an expert in your field.

Community Engagement: Get involved in online forums, Facebook groups, or local events related to your industry. Being active and helpful can bring attention to your business.

Customer Reviews: Encourage happy customers to leave positive reviews online. People trust other people's experiences, making this a powerful tool.

How to Get Started with Brand Ambassadors

Identify Enthusiastic Customers: Look for customers who are already fans of your brand and might be interested in spreading the word.

Offer Incentives: While you might not be paying them, offering free products, discounts, or other perks can be a great way to say thank you.

Set Clear Expectations: Communicate what you hope they'll share about your brand. But remember, the key is for their endorsement to remain genuine.

Build Relationships: Your brand ambassadors should feel like part of the team. Keep them in the loop about new products and company news.

Conclusion: Your Brand's Best Friends

Brand ambassadors can be your business's best friends. They're a cost-effective way to expand your reach, build credibility, and humanize your brand. By combining the power of genuine endorsements with other free marketing strategies, you can create a buzz around your business that resonates far and wide. So, let's get out there and find those champions who are as excited about your business as you are. Together, we can make some noise and grow our businesses, one shared post at a time.

Alright, let's dive into the realness of it all. When I hit that one-year mark in my business journey, I made sure to lock in my Erie County and New York State MWBE Certification. I was ready to level up, bidding on projects left and right. And let me tell you, the moment I got that certification, it was like a floodgate opened – three contracts in a week, totaling over $1million, just like that. No, those contracts did not come from the clear blue sky, they gave from me putting in the work, bidding on contracts, learning the game, sitting at the feet of my father's business and learning. I was moving fast, trying to keep up, pulling in folks from my neighborhood, even ex-felons. I didn't care about their past; I cared about giving them a shot, training them up, and getting these projects off the ground.

But here's the thing – that rapid growth wasn't part of the plan. I didn't have the processes in place to handle it all. Payroll was hitting me hard, with thousands flying out every week. Projects weren't paying on time, and we had no backup plan. I was drowning, and nobody around me understood what I was going through. The pressure was on, and soon enough, the quality of our work started slipping. We lost a project, and with it, our bonding.

I felt like I couldn't breathe. How did it all go left so quick? I was supposed to be on top, but here I was, struggling in silence. Nobody knew the real deal, and I was too afraid to reach out for help. COVID was a slap in the face, forcing me to slow down and reassess. It was a chance to rebuild, to get things back on track.

Just when I thought I was finding my footing again, I had a so-called friend come at me sideways, saying my business wasn't legit anymore and that I wasn't making noise, just because I began working in silence. See, I was no longer interested in having my name in lights, my focus was on keeping money in the bank. My carpenters were paid upwards of $60/ hour based on the prevailing wage rates and there were 17 employees, not including myself. Weekly payroll, for my business, far exceeded $40,000 per week. Let's not forget insurances. Business continued to grow, and my guys had steady work. I was so happy about the steady work that I didn't pay attention to the smoke. I saw the smoke, but I kept working. Things kept moving fast. This would continue for months and months, and the amount of work we were being awarded was not slowing down. None of the people around me understood what I was going through. No one understood the issues that we were encountering. Why would I expect this guy, with his "little man syndrome" to understand. But you know what? I didn't let his comment shake me. I remembered that this same dude had his own share of failures. Including a failed business quite like the one I was operating successfully. I'm telling you a piece of my story so that you understand, people can be quick to tear you down, especially when you're a minority or a woman in the game. But you gotta rise above it. You gotta get back up, stronger and smarter than before.

And you know what? I did just that. I rebuilt, I refocused, and now I'm moving forward, aligned with my goals and ready to take on whatever comes my way. This leads us into the next chapter and I can't wait to me you there.

Chapter 15:

Rising from the Ashes: Turning Setbacks into Comebacks

The Rollercoaster of Entrepreneurship
The journey of entrepreneurship is filled with highs and lows, and I've had my fair share of both. In my first year of business, after securing my MWBE Certification, I was on cloud nine, ready to elevate my hustle to new heights. Little did I know, the universe had a rollercoaster ride planned for me.

The Surge of Success and Its Challenges
Right after getting certified, boom! I was awarded three big contracts back-to-back. This was it—the breakthrough I had been waiting for. But with great opportunities come great challenges. I had to gear up quickly; my reputation and brand were on the line. I hit the streets, gathering a crew from my neighborhood, many of whom were looking for a second chance, just like I was given. We provided them with the training, tools, and transportation they needed. It was a rush, and I was determined not to let this chance slip through my fingers.

But here's the thing—I hadn't planned for this level of growth. My business plan didn't cover this rapid expansion, and I was winging it, caught up in the excitement and the hustle. The work was rolling in, and I was thrilled to provide steady jobs for my team. However, I missed the warning signs. The financial strain of meeting payroll, delayed project payments, and not having a line of credit began to weigh heavily on us.

Facing the Fire

The situation spiraled. We were stretched too thin, and the quality of our work suffered. It was a hard pill to swallow when we were let go from a project, losing not just money but our reputation. It felt like I was watching my dream crumble before my eyes. The isolation was real; I didn't feel like I could share my struggles with other business owners for fear of appearing weak or becoming a target.

The Blessing in Disguise

Then, as if on cue, *the world paused*. COVID-19 brought everything to a halt, including my business. But this break was what I needed. It allowed me to *stop, breathe,* and *reset*. I took this time to reevaluate, restructure, and rebuild my business with a clearer focus and stronger foundation.

Criticism and Resilience

Navigating criticism, especially from within our community, can be tough. I remember a moment when a peer tried to diminish my efforts, suggesting I didn't have a "real" business anymore. But I learned that criticism often says more about the critic than it does about you. I chose to rise above, remembering that every challenge is an opportunity to grow.

Moving Forward: Lessons Learned

Preparation is Key: Always plan for growth, ensuring your business can scale smoothly without sacrificing quality or financial stability.

Openness to Change: Be ready to pivot and adapt. The ability to reassess and restructure can be your business's saving grace.

Community Support: Don't isolate yourself. Building a network of support among like-minded entrepreneurs can provide a lifeline during tough times.

Resilience: Above all, stay resilient. Criticism and setbacks are part of the journey. What matters is how you bounce back.

Rising Above

Facing *setbacks* and *criticism* can be daunting, but they also teach us valuable lessons about resilience, adaptation, and the importance of community. I've learned to embrace each challenge as a stepping stone to greater success. Remember, it's not about how many times you fall; it's about how many times you get back up. Let's keep moving forward, building better, smarter, and in alignment with our business goals. Together, we can weather any storm and emerge stronger on the other side.

"Embracing Guidance: The Role of Coaches and Mentors Through the Storm"

Alright, let's keep it real. We've been talking about riding through the highs and lows of running a business, dealing with setbacks, and turning those challenges into victories. Now, I want to touch on something crucial that can make this journey a bit smoother: the importance of having a business coach or mentor.

Why a Coach or Mentor?

Imagine having someone in your corner who's been where you are, someone who's navigated the ups and downs and can guide you through the maze. That's what a business coach or mentor brings to the table. They're not just advisors; they're your business's guiding stars, providing wisdom, insights, and sometimes the hard truths we need to hear.

Overcoming the Fear

I get it. Letting someone into the intricate details of your hustle can be scary. It's like saying, "Here's my dream; tell me what I'm doing wrong." But here's the flip side: this openness can unlock doors you didn't even know were closed. A coach or mentor doesn't just look at your business from the inside out; they see it from the outside in, offering perspectives you might miss when you're in the thick of it.

The Outside Looking In

One of the biggest advantages of having a mentor or coach is their ability to provide that outside perspective. They're detached from the emotional rollercoaster you're on and can offer unbiased advice. It's like having a bird's-eye view of your journey, spotting potential pitfalls and opportunities from a vantage point you might not have when you're on the ground, running day-to-day operations.

Finding the Right Fit

Not all mentors or coaches are created equal, and finding the right one is key. You want someone who:

- *Understands Your Industry:* They don't need to be from your exact niche, but a good understanding of your business landscape counts.
- *Shares Your Values:* This journey is personal, and having someone who respects and shares your core values makes a huge difference.
- *Challenges You:* A great coach or mentor pushes you out of your comfort zone. Comfort is nice, but growth happens in the stretch zones.

The Benefits are Real
- *Accountability:* They keep you on track, making sure you're not just dreaming big but acting big.
- Network Expansion: A good mentor or coach can introduce you to people and opportunities you wouldn't have access to otherwise.
- *Emotional Support:* They've been there. They know the struggles and can offer the emotional support and understanding that friends or family might not.

Incorporating Their Insights. Integrating the insights and advice from your coach or mentor into your business doesn't mean losing your autonomy. It means enriching your strategy with wisdom and experience. It's about taking what resonates, applying it, and sometimes, respectfully disagreeing. After all, it's your dream, and you have the final say.

Achieving Harmony in Hustle: The Essence of Work-Life Balance

Dear Visionaries and Trailblazers,

As we journey through the intricate dance of entrepreneurship, especially as African American men and women, the harmony between our professional and personal lives often seems like a melody yet to be mastered. The crescendo of responsibilities can sometimes overshadow the gentle hum of our personal needs, desires, and well-being. This final chapter is an ode to the art of balance, an essential refrain in the symphony of success.

The Weight of the World: A Look at the Stats

Recent studies have illuminated a concerning trend: a significant portion of entrepreneurs report high levels of stress, with a staggering 30% experiencing its physical manifestations, such as hypertension and chronic fatigue. For minority and veteran business owners, the pressures of disproving stereotypes and overcoming systemic barriers can add an additional layer of stress. This isn't just a personal health crisis—it's a societal alarm that calls for immediate action.

A Call to Action: Cultivating Balance

The pursuit of work-life balance isn't a solo endeavor; it's a collective symphony that requires the participation of every member of your business. As leaders, we must not only embody this balance but also advocate for an environment that nurtures it among our employees. Here's how:

Implement Flexible Working Arrangements: Embrace policies that acknowledge the diverse needs of your team, from flexible hours to remote work options.

Encourage Regular Breaks: Promote a culture where taking breaks is seen as a recharge, not a retreat.

Foster Open Communication: Create channels for expressing concerns and challenges related to workload and stress.

Key Takeaways: The Final Notes

As we close this chapter—and our journey together through "Black in Business"—let's reflect on the melodies we've created:

Resilience in the Face of Adversity: We've explored real-life challenges and the solutions that have led to breakthroughs, underscoring the importance of perseverance.

The Blueprint of Understanding: From navigating business contracts to mastering operations and processes, knowledge has been our greatest tool.

The Art of Recovery: Dealing with failure isn't the end of the story; it's a pivot to a new beginning.

Marketing on a Melody: We've learned to compose impactful narratives, even on a budget, connecting our stories with those we serve.

A Chorus of Support: Building a network of allies has amplified our strength, proving that together, we can overcome any obstacle.

Celebrating Each Step: Every small win is a note in the larger symphony of our success.

Encore: A Wrap-Up of "Black in Business"

As we bring the curtain down on this guide, remember that your journey in entrepreneurship is a living, breathing composition that continues to evolve. The challenges we face, from understanding the intricacies of business contracts to creating efficient operations, dealing with setbacks, and marketing with limited resources, are but stepping stones on the path to greatness. Let's not forget the power of celebrating every victory, no matter how small, and the strength found in a supportive community.

Creating a work-life balance is not just an individual endeavor but a legacy we build for our businesses, ensuring that they thrive as spaces of innovation, well-being, and prosperity. As a minority, women, and veteran business owners, our narratives are woven with resilience, creativity, and the unyielding belief in the possibility of what can be achieved when we balance the scales of work and life with grace and intention.

Thank you for taking this journey with **"Black in Business."** May the chapters of your stories be filled with success, balance, and joy, echoing the lessons we've shared and the community we've built together.

For us, the hustle is often more than just a means to an end—it's a testament to our resilience, creativity, and determination to create legacies that uplift our communities. Yet, in the midst of striving for success, it's crucial to remember that our well-being is the foundation upon which our dreams are built. Here's how we can cultivate a more balanced life:

Set Boundaries with Grace
In a world that seldom stops, setting boundaries is a revolutionary act of self-care. It's about defining where your work ends and where your personal life begins. This might mean:

Designating specific work hours, even if you're working from home or running a business that demands around-the-clock attention.

Learning to say no to requests that exceed your capacity or don't align with your priorities.

Creating rituals that mark the beginning and end of your workday helps to mentally separate work from personal time.

Embrace the Power of Rest

Rest is not just a pause between work sessions; it's an active process of rejuvenation. African American entrepreneurs, especially, face unique stressors that can take a toll on our health. Prioritizing rest is not a luxury—it's essential.

Consider: Scheduling downtime in your calendar as you would any important appointment.

Finding restorative activities that bring you joy and relaxation outside of work, whether it's reading, spending time in nature, or engaging in a hobby.

Cultivate a Supportive Community

The journey of entrepreneurship can be isolating, but it doesn't have to be. Building a network of peers who understand the unique challenges and triumphs of running a business can provide:

- Emotional support, offering a space to share experiences, challenges, and successes.
- Practical advice, from managing finances to navigating business growth, that's grounded in shared experiences.

Prioritize Your Health

The correlation between stress and health issues, such as hypertension and anxiety, is particularly pronounced in our community. Incorporating healthy habits into your daily routine can significantly impact your overall well-being:

•Regular exercise, which can be as simple as daily walks, to reduce stress and improve physical health.

•Mindfulness practices, like meditation or deep-breathing exercises, enhance mental clarity and emotional resilience.

A Call to Action: Balance as a Legacy

Creating a work-life balance isn't just about improving our lives; it's about setting a precedent for future generations. By embodying these principles, we not only enhance our capacity to achieve our business goals but also model a way of living that values health, happiness, and fulfillment equally.

Let this be a call to action for each of us to invest in our well-being with the same fervor we apply to our businesses. Remember, achieving balance is not a one-time task but a continuous journey that evolves with our lives and ambitions.

Together, let's redefine the hustle by ensuring it sings in harmony with a well-lived life, creating a legacy of success that is both profound and sustainable. Here's to thriving in business and in life, with balance as our guiding melody.

Here's to crafting businesses that don't just succeed financially but flourish as beacons of health, happiness, and harmony.

With warmth and encouragement,

The MWBE Coach

Talia Johnson- Huff

Made in the USA
Middletown, DE
26 March 2024